Exploding
YOUR WEEKEND SERVICES

THE 10 REASONS KIDS COME TO CHURCH, AND HOW TO LEVERAGE THEM

TORNADO TWINS

Exploding Your Weekend Services:
The 10 Reasons Kids Come to Church,
and How to Leverage Them

by Tornado Twins

copyright ©2016 Tornado Twins

Trade paperback ISBN: 978-1-943294-51-0
Ebook ISBN: 978-1-943294-52-7

Cover design by Tornado Twins

Published by Kidmin Nation

Exploding Your Weekend Services is also available on Amazon Kindle, Barnes & Noble Nook and Apple iBooks.

CONTENTS

Introduction
WHAT IT'S ALL ABOUT

JESUS HAD NO PROJECTORS, no epic programs, no games, no music, no epic building—he was just a man walking around, teaching stuff. And people flocked to him! Children did too. So much so that Jesus' disciples wanted to keep the kids from going to Jesus.

When you read these gospel accounts, it's hard not to let out a deep sigh. You work so hard, you prepare all kinds of fun surprises for the kids, you teach what Jesus taught, you love them like Jesus did, but why aren't kids flocking to Jesus today?

Sometimes you descend into a pit of dark thought, and you think that you are the problem. Maybe there's something you still have to learn? Maybe God is keeping things from your ministry "because of your sins"? All these sad and useless thoughts fill your mind. You know they aren't true, but you still think about them.

Some children's ministers go so far as to say that you shouldn't want your ministry to grow. But that's not true either. God has given us the desire to reach all the people he made, not just a few. And the pain we feel about not reaching them is a pain that God gives. We can try to shut that pain off by changing our theology to an insiders-only theology, but that is not the answer either.

When we first started leading a children's ministry, there was no growth. We threw everything out and completely innovated a new model. And growth happened. Life change happened. After doing that for years, God called us to help other ministries. We've seen many ministries double in attendance, and some doubled multiple times. It wasn't the flash-in-the-pan gimmick type of growth. Kids and families really changed. They were local movements among the young. God was putting lives back together.

This booklet outlines 10 of the biblical methods we've used. You can implement them as you see fit. This doesn't mean your ministry will automatically grow. Nobody can promise you that. The Bible is clear about who does the planting and watering (us humans), and who gives the growth (he does). But it does mean that you'll be ready when God does send the growth. It means you may understand today's kids even better, and know what moves them.

The truth is that some of the methods used in children's ministry today are actually obstacles to reaching our modern-day culture. In our opinion, over half of the methods and philosophies taught at conferences today do not work, are incorrect, or are fully outdated. They're old methods dressed up with modern graphics and new buzzwords. But they aren't seen as such. They're still widely accepted, loved, and taught as new. This is the reason we started KidsWantAnswers.com and write books like these. We don't want you to be held back one bit. We want you and your ministry to get the boost of confidence and strength and encouragement and fresh methods that it deserves.

Secular culture has changed, worldwide. And it's ever-changing, like a tossing ocean. The gap between the church and the culture is widening, but only because we stay unmoved, frozen in place. We stand safely on the shores, rather than being like fishermen who go where the fish are. But it's so amazing to get in the boat and do so. The ocean isn't scary—it's beautiful, and it's under God's control. God created a wide open world out-side the walls of the church, and he wants us to explore it and bring it to him.

It's amazing to close the gap, and it's so easy to do once God shows you how. You already know some ways to do so, and we want to show you the methods and ideas that God has shown us. They've been wildly successful, and we can't wait to learn from how you do them, or what ideas you gain from them.

Let's pray that today's children's ministries all over the world learn to speak their current cultures' languages, in order to reach people with the timeless unchanging message of Christ.

In this book we won't start with what your children's min-istry needs or wants. There are plenty of books about that. We'll start with what the kids want. We'll describe the 10 main reasons kids come to church, and how your ministry can work with those motivations. Once you know them and capitalize on them, you will be able to take them further. You'll be start-ing where the kids are, so you can take them to where they need to be.

We pray this book blesses you and your ministry in many ways. We advise you to go through it with your team. The chap-ters are short and easy to read. You can easily go over a chapter a week and discuss the questions together. It's not just about what you'll read in this book; it's about unleashing the creativ-ity of your team. Have your team think along the lines of this book, and you might just take it further than we ever have.

Our goal is not to teach you what we've learnt. It's to have you go further than we have gone. It's to set your ministry on the fast lane, having it not only catch up with culture, but be in front of it, with Jesus at the wheel.

Let the children come to him,

— Ruben and Efraim Meulenberg

HOW TO READ THIS BOOK

THE LINE BETWEEN children's and youth ministry is a blurry one. There are a couple things I want to address before we get into the meat of this book. This book is about the 10 different types of kids we see in our church ministries and ways you can use that understanding to explode your children's ministry or your youth ministry—really, we prefer to talk about the two ministries together as one. We feel that they're often segregated, as if they're two different worlds, but more and more it's clear that really successful children's ministries are actually mini youth ministries.

Kids don't like stuff for kids; they like stuff for youth. This has proven itself over and over again. Actually, just last week we brought some kids from church to the movies and asked them what movie they wanted to see—they didn't choose *any* of the kids' movies. They chose serious adult movies. Not with inappropriate stuff necessarily, but I was like, "Man, that's boring even for me." But it's what they wanted. It's the same with video games—they want to play what their older brothers and sisters are playing.

In children's ministries, we have to sort of mimic this notion. So here, when we're talking about children's ministry, we're also talking about youth ministry and vice versa. Seeing it together as a whole helps you stay fresh. And you know, it's also about families. We're not a school system that segregates the children from the adults. School and church are two very different things, and church is for all ages!

DON'T FEEL OVERWHELMED.

Something else I want to mention before we get too far is that this book is going to be a bit of a fire hose. Some people want one point they can simmer on—that they can go over and mull over all day—but this is not that book. We're going to cover a mountain of topics and practical ideas here, and it might seem a bit overwhelming. Just know that you don't have to implement it all at once. It'll take time to build up the team and the systems to do this. To help you with this, we'll draw it all together at the end of the book, and come up with a way to implement the things that are covered.

If you look at any dish with all of its separate ingredients, it looks like a lot. *How did you know when to put this in? How do you know when to put that in?* It seems impossible until you look at the cookbook and see that if you take things step by step, the meal almost creates itself. It's the same with these ideas. Don't try to implement them all at once and just dump them into your children's ministry. It will be a mess! At the same time, don't hold back from trying any of them either; otherwise, things will only stay the same and become a tradition, which will be impossible to change without a lot of pain.

At the end, we'll give you some tips on how to slowly implement these ideas, but first, we're just going to give you a massive list to get you thinking. You're going to want to scream—but just enjoy that. If it's a fire hose, let's have a water fight!

WE'RE COVERING METHODOLOGY, NOT THEOLOGY.

This is a book about methodology and approach. You know, the way to do stuff. It's not about theology. I'm not going to slam a ton of verses at you; I mean, I trust that you are well versed in your theology. You don't need another book telling you to trust God as you do your ministry—you already know that!

THE TYPE OF CHURCH THIS IS WRITTEN FOR.

There are two types of churches. Some churches have their weekend services for a more Christian crowd and have separate programs to reach non-Christians. Other churches want their weekend services to be both for "insiders" and "outsiders." This book will be a good fit for the second. If you want your children's and youth services to be for both Christians and non-Christians, this book is for you.

We're aiming to turn your services inside out—without changing them too drastically—to make the message spill out into the community. That's the goal of this book.

It's not necessarily a prideful thing that you want people to talk about your ministry or especially what God is doing through it. Actually, it's a good thing. We see it in the gospels all the time. If we look at Jesus' ministry, you can see that everybody talked about it:

- "The news about him spread throughout the surrounding region." Luke 4:14 (BSB)
- "News of this spread through all that region." Matthew 9:26 (NIV)
- "And the news about him spread throughout the surrounding area." Luke 4:37 (NIV)
- "But they went out and spread the news about him all over that region." Matthew 9:31
- "This news about Jesus spread throughout Judea and the surrounding country." Luke 7:17 (NIV)

Good news is made to be spread, and your ministry spreads the good news. So it's a good thing when both the news and the news about the messenger spread throughout your region. In fact, that's what we're called to do—to bring the good news.

And that's what this book is about.

WHO IS "WE" AND WHO IS "ME"?

This book is written in both the "me" and the "we" form, which may be confusing if you don't know who the me's and we's are. When it says "me" it refers to Ruben. I'm the one of the twins who penned the book down. Yes, nice to meet you as well.

What's that? Oh, you're wondering what my twin brother was doing while I wrote the book? Actually, I have no idea. Let's ask him when we see him.

Kidding of course. He kept KidsWantAnswers.com running in order to serve youth and children's ministers worldwide.

So you guessed it. When this book refers to "we," it's both of the twins. Yes, twins are weird in that they use "me" and "we" interchangeably. If any non-twin does this, you should be asking questions about his sanity.

Lastly, sometimes "we" refers to the full team at *KidsWant Answers.com.*

Okay, that was more than enough preparation. Are you ready to start? Let's do this!

Chapter 1
GOD IS DOING SOMETHING NEW

FORGET ABOUT YOUR EXPERIENCE

GOD IS DOING SOMETHING NEW. As you might know, we've traveled to many different places and have seen many different methods of ministry. One book isn't enough to talk about all of the things we've seen. We could boast about our experience, but it matters little. Because the main thing we've come away with is that we all have to be prepared to do something new. We can't just stay comfortable and do what we've always done. That would turn God's living organism—called the church—into a ritualistic, lifeless tradition—called religion.

I grew up in Europe, and traditional churches aren't doing very well there. There is, however, a wave of new, young, vibrant churches that are just exploding—like the ICF churches and others. These churches have thrown out a lot of traditions. When it comes down to the possibility of improving our ministries, one thing we have to watch out for is our experience. Our experience is also our tradition, and our traditions can hold us back. My brother and I have been doing children's ministry for 17 years and constantly catch ourselves saying, "I don't think this is going to work because my experience tells me it won't." But then when we try it, we find that it actually *does* work.

Experience comes from the methods we've learnt, these methods come from the philosophies we have, and these philosophies come from asking questions. Sometimes we have to go all the way back to asking questions again. Wouldn't you agree?

So let's take a moment and go back to a very fundamental question that can put us on the path to improving our children's and youth ministries—a question once asked but now long forgotten:

What makes kids want to come to church?

Hold on—doesn't the Holy Spirit draw people toward himself?

Yes, of course. He alone draws people toward himself. This is the theological answer to the question. And at church, people get to experience God, get to know about God, get to accept God, grow in their friendship with God, and so on. So it's still a good question to ask. "What makes kids want to come to church?" Although it's not the only question we could ask, this is the question this book answers.

It's important to note that it doesn't say, "How do we get kids to come to church?" No, it's not about what you and I do. This book is about the kids' own motivation to come to church. It's "what makes kids *want* to come to church?" It's often baffling how little we talk about the kids' motivation in children's ministry. We just quietly accept that parents bring the kids and that's that. Let's go a step further and look at what actually motivates the kids themselves. When you understand and work with kids' own motivations, things will go a lot easier and you'll see an excitement in your ministry that you never thought was possible. The joy of ministry quadruples and then some, because you're working with what God has placed in kids' hearts!

It's also important to note that the question of this book is not the only kid-evangelism question we should be asking. For instance, kids can also find God *outside* of church. When you go into the community and help families, do outreach, or even train your own kids to reach other kids, you're also doing evangelism to the next generation.

We can recognize two types of evangelism, based on Jesus' words. There's "come and see" and there's "go and tell." This book is all about the come and see. The go and tell side of things fills an entire new book we hope to write one day. When you combine both come and see and go and tell, you're obeying Christ's commands. And boy is it amazing to see what God does when we obey those two tiny phrases.

WHAT MOTIVATES KIDS ANYWAY?

In children's ministry, we have a bit of a privilege that youth ministry doesn't have, which is that kids are brought by their parents and don't always have a choice as to whether they're going to come to church or not. Youth ministry—especially with kids old enough to drive—doesn't have that advantage. But this isn't an advantage we should be utilizing at all. Ever. We really need to ask ourselves: What can we do and how can we teach in a way that really impacts the lives of these kids? What makes them not want to miss a week of church? We want them to continue to go to church, so we need church to have some sort of solid effect on their daily lives. It can't just be about boring teaching.

In children's ministry, we tend to get a little lazy. I mean, let's be honest here. Sometimes we can't help but say to ourselves, "Well, these kids are just being brought by their parents, so all we have to do is teach them what God has for them." If teaching them is simply doing what the curriculum tells us, it often keeps us from thinking about what the kids actually need to learn. We're just following a script.

And that's why, ultimately, it's essential that we go back to the question, "Why do kids want to come to church?" With the answers to this question, you can use any curriculum out there and still make it have a more encompassing impact on kids' lives.

TEN REASONS KIDS *WANT* TO COME TO CHURCH

Thinking about this for years, we found 10 reasons why kids want to come to church. We call these the 10 motivations—because that's what they are—10 motivations kids have to come to church.

We didn't find any more than these 10. In fact, any new motive we found was simply one of the existing answers said in a different way. So we feel these 10 are quite encompassing. However, children's ministry is an ever-changing thing. It morphs, adapts, evolves. As children change and as ministries change, we'll definitely find more reasons why kids want to come to church. You'll see how that works later in the book. So you should always be looking out for more motivations. Add them to your plan of attack. And if you find more of them, let us know! We want to learn from you as well. But for now, these 10 are quite encompassing for our day and age, and they will give you a ton of great insights and practices. You may find more practices than you can currently implement. In that case, focus on amplifying the ones that align with your ministry's strengths. Add the others over time. It'll all become clear toward the end of the book.

TAKING THINGS FURTHER

TEAM QUESTIONS

Note: The team questions do more than revisit what's taught in the chapter. They help you take things further than the chapter did. Some things are better discovered by yourself, and as a team. Wouldn't you agree?

1. In the gospels we read the story of parents who brought their kids to Jesus. In this case, it doesn't say if the kids were motivated to come themselves. It only says the parents brought the kids. What motivates your church's parents to bring their kids?

2. Are your kids as motivated to come to church as the parents are to bring them?

3. Let's be gut-honest; have you ever been "guilty" of assuming that kids will be brought by their parents, rather than working with kids' own motivations to come to church?

4. What are some of the motivations kids have to come to church? How many can you think of?

5. When you were a child, what motivated you to come to church?

6. It's also good to look at the obstacles kids face. What are some of the reasons they would NOT want to come?

7. When you were a child, what were the reasons you did not want to attend church at times?

8. Spend some time in prayer, asking God to raise kids' desire for him. That they would—as the psalmist said—thirst for God like a deer pants for water. In the end, we cannot change people's motivations. Only God can. All

we can do is recognize them, work with them, and pray that God will turn these motivations toward himself. You can also pray for God's wisdom in understanding the latest generation that he so expertly created and put in our care.

Chapter 2
THE LEAST-MOTIVATED KIDS

EACH MOTIVATION THAT KIDS HAVE to come to church has a certain level of commitment attached to it. We'll start with the lowest level of commitment and make our way through the higher levels.

Here's a nice little pyramid graphic for your viewing pleasure. Pictures don't have to be for kids only, right?

THE DROP-OFF KID

MOTIVATION 1: THE DROP-OFF KID

We'll start at the bottom corner, where we have what I like to call "the drop-off kid." That name is pretty straightforward, right?

This is the kid who is literally being dropped off at church. It's possible that they don't even want to be there, and this tends to be the lowest level of commitment in a kid's heart. It could also be that their commitment is simply not yet known. Not to you, and not to them. They're just dropped off, and that's that.

The parents or grandparents who bring these kids might have a higher level of commitment (which is likely, seeing as they are indeed bringing their kid in the first place), but the kids themselves are generally not particularly motivated to attend church. It's really important to realize that there are different *levels* of motivation when it comes to attending church, but we'll get more into that later.

SO WHAT MOTIVATES THIS TYPE OF KID?

The motivation for the drop-off kid is "my parents or grandparents brought me." Aaaaaand that's about it! That's all. It may be what they're used to. Or it may be new to them. Maybe they don't really have a say in the matter.

There are a lot of children's ministries that operate in this corner and don't even glance at the other nine levels of motivation. Needless to say, we could really benefit from breaking out of that.

THE DROP-OFF KID IN THE BIBLE

The Bible gives us a fair amount of reference material when it comes to understanding what motivates people to attend services, so I'm going to try to make these connections as often as possible. In the case of the drop-off kid, we can think about the parents who brought the kids to see Jesus. The disciples tried

CASE STUDY:
ASKING A BOLD QUESTION

For about two months, I was on a secret mission. I would talk with as many kids as possible at church. I'd move from open chair to open chair and talk with them while the service was going on. I'd say, "Okay, I've got a totally honest question for you. If you're really, really honest, would you rather be here, or somewhere else?" About 50 percent of kids wanted to be elsewhere. Of that 50 percent, half of them wanted to be at a theme park, the other half wanted to be playing videogames (yes, this includes the girls).

Now this is not a fully fair or accurate measurement. By asking the question this way, I essentially said, "Hey, think of the coolest thing you could be doing right now and tell me what it is." Of course kids' imaginations go to the most fun places and pastimes. But still, it's eye-opening to ask this question and to see kids' honest responses. No amount of reading gets you to know your kids as well as talking to them.

Needless to say, we made some changes after this little test. In later teaching series, we didn't only see a surge in kids' motivation, we saw over 30 percent growth in attendance. We had lines going out the door and we couldn't handle the check-in fast enough. But we wouldn't have gotten there if we hadn't done some soul-searching first. Not just our souls, but also those of the kids we serve.

to hold them back, but Jesus corrected them, saying, "Let the children come to me."

This example doesn't exactly address whether the kids wanted to go to Jesus, but it does say specifically that it was the parents who brought them. And Jesus certainly does say, "Let the children come to me." So, it's very likely that the kids really want to go meet this famous miracle-maker, but we do not know. The fact remains that if their parents hadn't brought them, they probably wouldn't have been there. And that still remains the key for the drop-off kid—it's the motivation of the one who brings them, not of the ones who are brought.

AMPLIFYING THIS LEVEL OF MOTIVATION

Each level of motivation is something you can work with. It's something you can recognize and then try to amplify. Look at it this way: we are only human, so we cannot create something out of nothing. However, we can encourage and grow what's already there. So by recognizing a level of motivation, and then encouraging and planning for it, you help kids become more motivated for church. You are literally working with what you've got. Or better, with what *they've* got.

Once you've gone over all types of motivations, you can evaluate your ministry based on them. You can evaluate your own interactions with kids and teenagers as well. And you can plan ahead. When you're planning a new teaching series or a summer outreach program, plan your promotion based on these 10 motivations. In order to help you do so, I'll be telling you practical ideas we've used for each motivation.

So how can you amplify the type of motivation possessed by the drop-off kid?

Well in this case the motivation is on the side of the one bringing the kid. One way to amplify this is to connect with parents and grandparents:

1. A common way is to send a letter home to the parents or grandparents with some information about the series you're working on at the time.

2. A step further would be to put up some posters or flyers in the area where parents or grandparents walk through to drop off or pick up their kids. Try to get them involved in what their kids are doing in your children's ministry. At the very least, keep them in the loop.

3. Actually, the best way to do that is with a trailer. Play a trailer for the adults either before or after a service with a little information about the series you're about to do with their kids. If it's a really cool series, then the trailer can be really cool as well. If you don't have a pre-made trailer or aren't sure how to go about making your own, you can take a look at our website, KidsGotAnswers. com, to get some ideas. There are different lengths, such as 30 seconds or 1 minute, or you can even try slides. A lot of churches use slides because they're pretty straightforward, and they're also great visual tools to keep the parents informed.

4. Next is a more personal approach. When you see people bringing kids, encourage them. Especially when it's not their own kids. I remember the grandfather who broke down during a conversation I had with him after he dropped off his grandson. I remember the conversation with a mother whose three popular kids constantly brought friends. I told her that her home was a magnet, and she then made it her goal to have kids sleep over at her house each week, so that she could bring them to church. She kept this up for years. She proceeded to invite me and my twin brother to her kids' birthday parties as well, so we could meet befriended families. We connected with dozens and dozens of parents and kids, many of whom started coming to church. All of this started with just one conversation.

PRO TIP:

Look at the first three methods above, and compare them to the last one. The first methods are "mass market" methods. The last is personal and specific. Too often, we stick to the first three only. These are good—especially the trailers, they break through all the noise—but we cannot forget the personal approach. I cannot stress enough that you should think outside of what you can plan. Have your hands free and your tasks off your plate so that God can put random conversations into your schedule. If you ever heard us speak at conferences, you know the question we always ask, "How much ministry will be done if your programs were removed?"

PRO TIP 2:

If you look at the kind of promotional stuff we have, you'll notice that it's more youth-oriented—it doesn't feel childish. We do this on purpose and we encourage you to do the same, regardless of what curriculum or material you use. This plays into what we were discussing earlier about kids preferring things with a bit of an "older" feel to them, but also, this information is for the parents too. We really don't want it to be dumbed down with finger paints and such. No finger paints please! I'm sure parents will appreciate that too.

Additional options to amplify the commitment of this type of kid are invite cards, which is a bit more traditional but can still work. However, I would suggest this method only for ministries based in America. In Europe, there's currently a backlash toward organized religion, and an invite card isn't always likely to go over well. In the States, though, you can go for it. But let's think this through for a second, shall we? I remember being a junior higher and there was this girl I liked but I didn't really know her. One day she came up to me—just me!—and I got all hopeful. She then gave me an invite card to something from her church. She said, "You should come," and then left. I didn't know if I should feel happy or sad. My eyes followed her, and I saw her give it to others as well. I obviously felt a little less special. So I gathered the courage to ask her what it was about. She told me it was from her church and if she gave out enough invite cards, she'd get some sort of reward. All that was left of my positive image of her just crumbled right there. I was a pawn in the scheme of her church. No relationship was involved.

Did her method work? I don't know. It may have. There's a lot of spammy marketing that works. And if it did, my case against it might not hold up. But I seriously doubt this method.

Fast-forward four years and I was leading my first children's ministry. The preteen ministry. I was only 17 and only had three volunteers. (Hey, it was a small church! Don't judge!) I asked my volunteers how we would have kids invite other kids and they said, "Give them invite cards? Maybe give a prize to the kid who gives out the most?" Needless to say, my inner junior higher screamed. I decided to do a year without invite cards, just to see if we'd be creative enough to come up with other solutions. We didn't lose any growth! Instead of giving invite cards, we'd do all kinds of crazy stuff to help kids remember the event and invite others. I even made a song with the day and time in it that kids remembered years after.

All this to say, invite cards might be just the thing for you. They may work really well. But if they don't, scratch them off the board, allowing for new creative methods. Or make them really special—make them look like exclusive tickets or something. Okay, I better stop before this book turns into a brainstorm.

NOTES

How this works: Once you find the answers in the chapter, you can note them here for future reference. Also capture your own ideas. You'll often get ideas while reading, which you'll never think of again. So capture them now and implement them over time!

1. Motivation 1 = the d _____ o _____ kid

2. Their motivation is: "My _____ me"

3. Ways to amplify this motivation:

4. Your own ideas to amplify this motivation:

TAKING THINGS FURTHER

TEAM QUESTIONS

Note: The team questions do more than revisit what's taught in the chapter. They help you take things further than the chapter did. Some things are better discovered by yourself, and as a team. Wouldn't you agree?

1. How do you currently connect with parents?

2. How could you better connect with parents—both as a ministry as well as personally?

3. Are your hands free enough to have God interrupt you with unplanned conversations (with both parents and kids)?

4. The chapter told the story of how Ruben removed an option (invite cards) so that more creative options would be found. Which thing could you remove? For how long will you remove it?

5. Assignment: Find a few people who do not attend church. It doesn't matter if they're kids or not. Just find someone you're comfortable talking to. Now ask them what would make them go to church. Would they want to be invited? Would church need to change? Tell them you're not there to change them, but to ask their opinion. Whatever they say, value their opinion. What did they say and what could you learn from it for children's ministry?

6. Did you have a crush in junior high as well? (This has absolutely nothing to do with what this book is about, but why not recall some fun stories?)

7. Is your ministry better at "mass market" methods (such as posters, trailers) or at personal and specific methods? Which of the two would you need to grow in?

8. Spend some time in prayer, asking God to soften the hearts of drop-off kids. Also ask him to show you who are bringing their kids to church, and which of them you should encourage.

Chapter 3
THE KIDS WHO SAY "YES"

ANOTHER TYPE OF COMMITMENT we often see in our ministries is the invited kid.

The invited kid is, to avoid a more convoluted explanation, the one who was invited by a friend. They weren't forced by their parents or grandparents to come to church—they've actually agreed to the idea of attending. It's a slightly higher level of motivation, which is kind of funny because it's usually a drop-off kid who brings in the invited kid, and then the invited kid tends to be higher on the commitment scale.

Think about that for a moment. We often feel that the longer someone attends church, the higher his or her commitment level is. But that idea is completely false. Often, those who are new to church have a higher commitment level. Things are fun and exciting to them. In the Western world we have a preconceived idea of a staircase model. People always start at the bottom of the stairs and then take steps of commitment. This model is bogus. For instance, those who just accepted Christ are better at reaching their non-Christian friends than those who've been Christians for 10 years. Why? Because the latter often lost their non-Christian friends, and the former has this new-life-with-Christ excitement.

Instead of the staircase model, people can appear and reappear anywhere on the map. Our own commitment can rise and fall in a matter of days. We can all be hungry for more of Christ, and we're all one decision away from being a cold Pharisee.

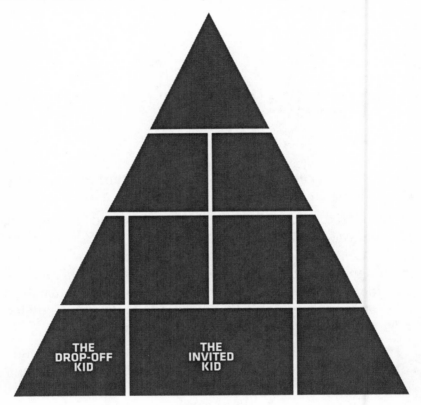

SO WHAT MOTIVATES THIS TYPE OF KID?

For the invited kid, their motivation will be, "My friend brought me." Fair enough, right? It's important to help these kids have a great experience at church. The case study below will illustrate that point.

THE "INVITED KID" IN THE BIBLE

The biblical example of the invited kid would be Peter, who was invited by Andrew to meet Jesus. I concede that in this case we're not talking about kids, but it's still a relevant example.

AMPLIFYING THIS LEVEL OF MOTIVATION

The way to amplify this type of motivation is simple: Help kids to invite their friends. In the last chapter, we went over the limits of invite cards. What you'll want to do is get things in kids' hearts and minds. You could challenge them to do a Saturday night sleepover, for example, and then have them bring their friends to church in the morning. You could throw a "bring your best friend to church" day in which you honor kids' best friends.

You can also get their parents involved in this. Some parents actually really enjoy it. You also have super connected families—you know, those families whose homes are always buzzing with activity, who always have friends coming over, and who are always serving people—a strong fellowship house. They can bring in a lot of kids as you saw previously.

I've made it a point to encourage them as much as possible and to let them know that they're really good at what they're doing. These parents often don't realize the potential they have, but they'll excel at it once you open their eyes to it. You saw an example of this previously. When you see families like that, be sure to talk to them about what they're doing. By making them excited, you're shooting one little arrow that can make a huge difference.

One thing I'd love to try soon is to give kids short videos that they can show their friends. This is the new invite card, if you will. It's a trailer of your church or of the series you'll be teaching at church. When made appealing enough, it'll have a huge effect, especially if kids can post (part of) it on social media. The sky is the limit!

LET'S GO FURTHER THAN "BRING YOUR FRIENDS"

A lot of times in children's and youth ministry, we say lines like, "Bring your friends! Bring your friends!" and that's it. We sound like a broken record and never really give them tools they can use to actually invite their friends. It's important to take it a step further.

Wouldn't it be better to actually show them *how* to invite friends? Or even have them practice inviting? Here's an easy way to do this, without needing to prepare anything. Simply ask kids, "How would you invite a friend to church?" Then have them give their examples. The kids who are good at this will be teaching the kids who aren't.

You could even go to a kid who was invited and say, "Who invited you, and how did they invite you?!" It's more helpful for them if we demonstrate how to do things instead of just telling them they should. This is a principle behind all teaching: don't just tell what they "ought to do"; show how they should; then have them copy you; then have them teach others.

"Invite your friends" is an "ought to do." It's better to say, "Invite them like this or like that." Also let them come up with examples, have them role play, and so on—those are how-to's.

We can summarize this chapter in two ways: find new ways for kids to invite kids; and find new ways to train kids to invite kids.

NOTES

How this works: Once you find the answers in the chapter, you can note them here for future reference. Also capture your own ideas. You'll often get ideas while reading, which you'll never think of again. So capture them now and implement them over time!

1. Motivation 2 = the i _____ kid
2. Their motivation is: "My _____ me"
3. Ways to amplify this motivation:

4. Your own ideas to amplify this motivation:

TAKING THINGS FURTHER

TEAM QUESTIONS

Note: The team questions do more than revisit what's taught in the chapter. They help you to take things further than the chapter did. Some things are better discovered by yourself, and as a team. Wouldn't you agree?

1. What's the one difference between the drop-off kid and the invited kid?

2. Have you seen commitment as a sequential process (a staircase), rather than the messy back-and-forth it really is? How does it make you look differently at new people and at those who've been at church for a longer time?

3. How can you improve your children's services for new people (not just for parents, but also for kids)? (It may even help to do a walk-through over your campus and facilities to see if they can easily find the way, feel accepted at each point, and so on.)

4. Have you told kids to invite their friends without telling them how? How could you train them to invite others? How could you make this training fun?

5. How did the story of Scott (the neighbor) impact you?

6. When was the last time you were a newcomer at a religious place? Have you ever visited a place of a different religion? Do you identify with the fear that new people may have?

7. We Christians often talk about God opening doors. But among church movements in China, people say, "If God doesn't open a door, he might open the window, or show us how to break through the wall." Does this view change

your view of how we can reach our neighbors for Christ? Who went through the window to invite you?

8. Pray for God to give the families of your church many connections and many open hearts. Pray that they'll use every opportunity to extend the invitation to know more about Christ.

Chapter 4
ENGAGING THOSE WHO ARE CREATURES OF HABIT

THE FINAL TYPE OF COMMITMENT on the bottom level of our triangle is the habitual kid.

In the same straightforward manner as the drop-off kid or the invited kid, the habitual kid simply has a habit of coming to church. This is a bit higher on the commitment scale as well; coming to church may not be a spiritual commitment in their hearts, but it's something they're used to, so they're going to keep doing it.

Even if their parents or grandparents wouldn't push them, they'd still go to church because that's simply what they're used to. They have learnt that this is a good thing, and in that sense, their commitment is higher than that of kids who aren't committed to this "good thing" of attending.

You know how certain personalities are more habitual than others? Some personalities *need* regularity. In some families, it seems like every single member of the family is like that. The more routine-oriented kids come every week, and their families come every week—that's what's normal for them. That's their level of commitment, and they're all right with it.

It doesn't take that much effort to help habitual people come to church. In fact, it hardly takes any effort at all. After all, it's already a habit for them. This is why we ministers spend more time helping non-committed people to come to church. This is obviously what we call outreach. We always need to do lots of outreach to reach only a few. This is best illustrated in Jesus' parable about the sheep. One sheep was lost so the shepherd left the 99 to find the one. When we're talking about the habitual folks, we're talking about the 99. They're perfectly fine when left behind for a while, so that you can reach the one.

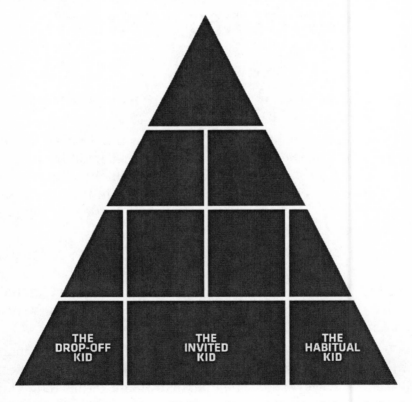

Now I know that saying this is quite controversial, and that's why reference Jesus' parable. If Jesus hadn't taught this parable, we wouldn't feel that leaving the 99 behind would be a Christian thing. I mean, it's 99 good, decent, committed people. Leaving them behind feels like neglect, but is it?

Think about it. The 99 sheep were grazing just fine. They're self-feeders. They have some form of maturity the one does not have. If we really think the 99 are dependent on us, then they're not the 99. They're the one. We should give the 99 some credit here. They know what to do. And when any of them become the one, you'll go after them.

HOW TO HAVE A CULTURE THAT'S OPEN TO OUTSIDERS

I see too many children's ministers hang out with the same kids each week. We all do it. It's easy. You know them, they know you. You love on them, and they give you love back. It feels good. It feels loving, because it is. It's a great joy in ministry and it is as God intended church to be, but the picture isn't complete. There are still many outside. This wonderful community God granted us to serve will slowly fade away unless you focus on the missing ones. The new kids. Focus on the families who aren't reached yet. Those who are confused, hurting, dirty—those who don't love you back.

The reward for returning the one is incredible. But too few of us actually do it. As ministry leader, talk to your volunteers. Do they hang out with the same kids each week? Let them think of ways to include new kids. To not form cliques—closed groups—who know so much about one another that it repels newcomers.

To be honest with you, I don't think I've ever been able to get more than 50 percent of the volunteers to not be clique-based. Most will form cliques and stick with them. They'll call it "fellowship" or "deeper discipleship," and they have a point, but it's also familiarity. And for many, familiarity is why they serve.

Luckily, you don't have to change everyone. In order to truly have a culture that welcomes outsiders, we often just focus our energy on those volunteers who truly have a heart for outsiders. You simply can't change everyone. And you don't have to.

So how do you have a culture that's open to outsiders, and how do you keep this culture? We've come to these conclusions:

- If you want your church or ministry to be open to outsiders, you always have to push against clique-behavior. You can do this by constantly teaching and training on hospitality.

- However, you must realize you will always have clique-behavior. It just can't become the norm and take over the culture. Cliques are like clumps in the soup—they'll be there and you best keep stirring so they won't take over.

- The way to have an open culture is to train those who are open to outsiders. (This is also the stirring of the soup.) You can try to change those who aren't, but it only causes disagreements, anger, misunderstanding, and drama. Let them be, but don't let them take over.

- So in short: (A) constantly teach and train for openness-to-outsiders, setting a culture that expects and rewards outreach; (B) have a committed army of those who engage new kids; and (C) many will never do it but they'll at least know it, and they add value to your ministry in other ways. Let them be, but don't allow them to turn the culture inward (which brings you back to A).

SO WHAT MOTIVATES THIS TYPE OF KID?

These kids are motivated by the idea that "church is what we do." Maybe you would like a stronger motivation than that, but this is okay too. A biblical example is the people who went to a synagogue or to the temple as part of their weekly habit.

AMPLIFYING THIS LEVEL OF MOTIVATION

Amplify this type of motivation by teaching church attending as a spiritual habit. That's what it is! This is also one of the habits we teach in our curriculum series, "S.O.S." Each week, kids follow the story of a guy who is stranded on a deserted island. While they follow his story, kids learn the habits that are needed for more than survival—they are the habits you need in order to stay close to God. You probably have a similar series in which you address the same ideas (if not, you can get "S.O.S." at www.KidsWantAnswers.com).

It's important for kids to know that it's not biblical to stay away from the services. We are to meet with each other and build each other up. That's the biblical model. But when you look at that model, you see how many of today's children's ministry's practices don't fit it. See, if all ages are the church, then kids are the church as well. And if we are to build each other up, then kids are to build others up as well. But if our services are built to only teach kids the way a school does, then kids don't have anything to contribute themselves. They just attend in order to be built up, not to build someone else up. They're not expected to bring anything, only to receive something. And this creates a generation of consumers, not active church participants. The school model simply isn't biblical.

NOTES

How this works: Once you find the answers in the chapter, you can note them here for future reference. Also capture your own ideas. You'll often get ideas while reading, which you'll never think of again. So capture them now and implement them over time!

1. Motivation 3 = the h_____ kid
2. Their motivation is: "_____"
3. Ways to amplify this motivation:

4. Your own ideas to amplify this motivation:

TAKING THINGS FURTHER

TEAM QUESTIONS

Note: The team questions do more than revisit what's taught in the chapter. They help you to take things further than the chapter did. Some things are better discovered by yourself, and as a team. Wouldn't you agree?

1. Could there be those who have a habitual level of commitment, but still don't attend each week? How so or how not so?

2. Are you better at finding the one or shepherding the 99?

3. When a mason is done with his work, he has built the wall and he's proud of it. But it would be strange if he camped out next to his wall and couldn't leave it. Could the same be said for ministry? Once there are self-feeding Christians in your church, is it healthy to keep pampering them? In what way does *leaving* those you've served benefit those you've served?

4. Evaluate how open your ministry's culture is to outsiders.

5. Do you have a "clique" in children's ministry? Remember, it's not bad to have a group of kids who prefer to hang out with you. You can actually keep this group around you and use this small community to receive new kids. As long as you lead your kids to do so. But your group becomes a clique the moment it's harder to receive outsiders. Have you used excuses such as "we're just going deep right now" or "we built something this year, having a new kid would affect that"?

6. Is your heart truly broken for those who don't know Christ yet?

7. No, is it really?

8. Pray for two things—those outside the church who need the good news, and your regular, habitual kids. Pray that the latter will be willing to bring and be hospitable to new kids.

Chapter 5
SEEING THE JOY OF YOUR MINISTRY RISE

NOW WE'VE ARRIVED at the first motivation that's one level up. The bottom level motivations are what we'd call external motivations. These motivations don't necessarily come from the kids. They come from the parents or the expectations of culture.

This next level up will show kids' *internal* motivations. These motivations are self-motivated. It's the reason kids themselves are motivated to come to church. And this is where it gets fun.

It's important to point out that many children's ministries never get to see kids of this level of motivation and higher. Many ministries have become used to serving the drop-off kids, the occasionally invited kid, and the habitual kid. Sometimes, these three are the only motives you can find among the kids and families.

Sure, you sometimes see kids temporarily skyrocket up a few levels, but it often doesn't last long. Kids often have these periods where they're spiritually very excited, but then sink back to the bottom three levels. If you see this happening in your ministry, don't get depressed just yet. I've seen it happen in ours as well. It takes time and tons of intentionality to raise the bar, and to see more kids who have the upper seven motivations.

Now let's be gut-honest here. Here's the stuff you often don't read in books: the truth is that sometimes it doesn't happen at all. Sometimes you never see the upper seven levels, and kids are always more or less forced to go to church. There are a couple of reasons for this. As the ministry leader, sometimes you just won't get the room to execute the vision. Other times you do, but the families who attend have settled for a lower commitment, regardless of what you do. I'm not telling you this to discourage you. On the contrary, you need to know it isn't always your fault! Ministry is a team sport, and you might be an incredible top-scorer, but you can't win alone—unless God miraculously decides that you can.

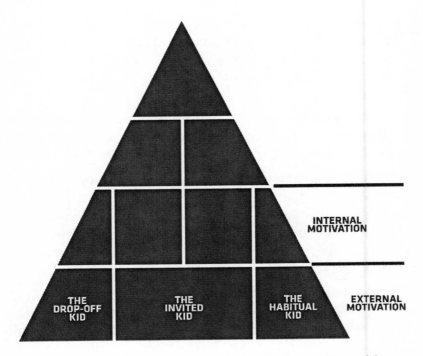

I've been in ministries where I simply knew I would never be able to take the ministry further. Yes, I said it. It shouldn't be controversial to admit this. Didn't Jesus say he sometimes takes the candle away from a church? You don't get to decide whether the candle is there or not. And you're certainly not judgmental when God has quietly revealed to you that the candle is gone. See, in these cases, I knew that God had me move on to the next ministry. But sometimes it would take time before he'd show me which next ministry. In these desert-periods, I would still serve him, but in a different way. I'd make sure the children's ministry ran as best as it could, but I wouldn't bleed for it. In a place that's as flexible as a rock wall, it's a lot easier when God has not called you to make a change. What I'd do instead is serve the few families who really wanted to grow, and didn't stress over the overall culture of the ministry.

CASE STUDY: WHEN THE CHURCH IS ALL TALK

At times we've found ourselves at a church that was all talk, no walk. We'd never say this out loud, because it's not right to be negative about a church. But in our hearts, we'd know and plan accordingly.

For the time God had us live there, we'd do our own outreach. We'd go to the skate parks, the sport parks, the community barbeques, the town concerts. We'd meet with families we knew and we'd organize fun outings to theme parks where kids could take their friends. A whole new ministry would emerge outside of the church, one that wasn't officially part of any church. We couldn't take these new kids to a church that's all fake and all talk. For as long as God had us there, we'd serve him with all our hearts. But mostly off the record.

We have to ask ourselves, what is the church anyway? Is it a non-profit that's registered at your church building's address? No, the church is the people of God. It's you and I. And we can serve God in any capacity, official or unofficial.

In some rare cases we had kids from our outside unofficial ministry come into the church and help us out. They'd be serving the church while not even being part of it. In those cases we'd teach them the downside of Phariseeism as they could see it all around them. In some of those cases the kids who served with us were not even Christian yet. They'd see the difference between our lives and that of a church body that was dead inside. It would make them think, "If I choose to become a Christian, what kind of Christian will I become?" And some have indeed chosen to become the correct type of Christian later.

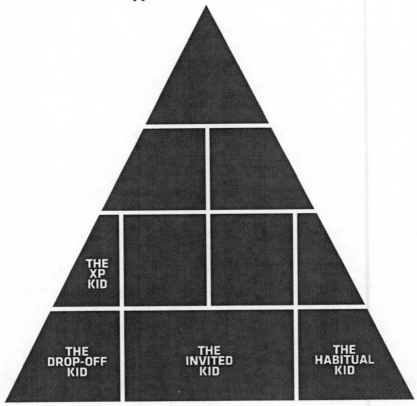

As you see, you can always serve God, anywhere. But for His sake, don't stay at such a church for too long! Your qualities have better uses in God's kingdom.

HERE IS WHERE IT GETS FUN

The first motivation that is self-motivated is that of the experience kid. This is the type of kid who comes to church for the experience, and the experience could be so great that it spills over into the community and makes other kids want to come as well, attracting more experience kids.

Now, before I delve into this, I want to address something you may have wondered about in the past. It's sort of a theological battle: if you make church a better experience, are you, in essence, just being gimmicky? No, you aren't. You're just being hospitable. It's important for you to realize that if you want to reach a certain type of people, you have to speak their language, and language is also about style. So sometimes you have to change your style so that it reaches out to kids in your environment. I'd say that about every ten years or so the kid culture changes, so it's pretty important that you update your style along with it. With every series that we do at KidsWantAnswers.com, we also have to change the structure of the program a little so that kids never really know what to expect. If it's constantly the same thing, kids already know, "Okay, here comes the Bible verse, here's the Bible story, now a recall game, now a workshop, now this, or now that," and if it's the same thing every time, kids get bored. And if they're bored, then their experience won't be something that spills out into the community.

So how can we make a great experience for kids in church?

Well, we wrote another book on that for you, but here's the short version. When I first started leading a children's ministry in Europe, we didn't have the great resources that a lot of English-speaking nations have—America and the UK have some really great stuff—so we had to create our own. We looked at lots of models, but we felt that the European culture was just a bit too secularized compared to the American culture and many materials didn't work. We had to really raise the bar.

So we ended up working with some fantastic Hollywood writers and constructing the epic story, which I want to tell you about here, if you aren't already familiar with it, because it has really changed the experience for the children in our ministries. The story continues with every lesson and—much like the parables of Jesus—each lesson has teachings woven into it. The program basically flows out of following the story. Every week the story ends with a cliffhanger, and every week the story gets crazier and crazier, raising the stakes, just like any great film.

I once had a friend mention to me that any series longer than four weeks doesn't really work. After about three weeks, he said, the excitement of a series tends to wear off. This is certainly true when the curriculum is not written in a way that keeps things in a state of perpetual suspense. So we started shaping our curriculums with a certain level of suspense, and now we find that kids are actually sad when the series ends. They want more. So now we're even starting to come up with Part II or Part III of some series!

It's these ongoing variables—these series with every episode, every week, raising the stakes—that really draws in the experience kid.

When we developed this model at our kids' ministry in Europe, the number of kids doubled almost overnight. It was incredible. Kids didn't even want to go on vacation! No joke—they were begging their parents not to go because they didn't want to miss a week of church. And that first series we created back then wasn't even particularly special—it still had an effect though.

Later there was also a church we worked at in America that had 3,000 kids, a mega church by all accounts, and once we updated the experience with these stories, we grew about 30 percent in two months. Those numbers and examples show that when you draw in the experience kids, a whole lot of kids come with them. It's a huge next step.

I really feel that narrative and story are the language of today's culture. Culture is so much faster now, and kids are on their phones constantly, so you need something that helps keep their focus over a longer period of time. Story still does that. And since Jesus used story all of the time, we can learn from him to see how he did it.

Earlier I told you about the story series called "S.O.S." Another example is a story we're in the process of making right now, and it's probably one of the biggest we have so far: "Future Spies" is a spy story that continues every week with different groups of spies conducting missions. It's based around the idea that Jesus gives us missions for our daily lives and that we have to execute them; we way not understand the mission he has given to someone else compared to the mission he has given us. So there's some rivalry between the spies that shows this really well. Eventually, they find a common villain who is trying to stop their missions, and they unite and work together. It's an action story with special effects and everything, and it's a lot of fun. And kids love it.

We constantly encourage other ministries to develop series like these, should they have the means to. A few churches already started doing so for their own congregations. If you have the time and resources to do so, go right ahead! If not, you can find these series available for you on our website (KidsWantAnswers.com).

We're constantly making series in this manner with this sort of narrative style. It's important to note that this kind of storytelling is essential for other levels of motivation as well, but we'll talk about that more later. And it's important to have a variety of stories, not just one flavor or one type.

We taught some of these principles a year ago at a children's pastors' conference, and last week a church sent us a trailer of their own narrative series. They thanked us for inspiring them to do this and were stoked about the results. It was so awesome. They were inspired by these same points and were able to make it happen. It's a huge amount of work, but if you're able to do it, go for it. How exactly you do it doesn't matter— you can be really creative!

PRO TIP:

Businesses create great experiences in order to attract customers. Churches create excellent experiences because the joy of the good news reverberates in their hearts, and they wish to share it with the world. Whenever God's word is rediscovered, there is an explosion of love and joy, and the church serves others out of that love and joy, and this creates an excellent experience. True experience isn't manufactured—it is lived out.

AMPLIFYING THIS LEVEL OF MOTIVATION

For the experience kid, the motivation is, "I want to see how the story continues" or "I want to experience this thing." The first step is to have an experience that kids will talk about throughout the week, such as an ongoing narrative curriculum that has a high level of engagement and grows in intensity over the course of the series.

Other things you can do to amplify this type of commitment is give them some sort of media for their home. This helps re-emphasize the lesson and, moreover, gets the experience out into the community immediately. Now be careful, because homework is not cool. A lot of times we basically give kids a sheet with assignments, which is homework in their eyes, and these sheets rarely make it home, if they even make it as far as the trash can (we've all seen the sheets floating around under chairs and strewn on tables).

We've replaced them with handouts that have unlock codes. In some series kids can unlock a level of a videogame; in others they can watch the series' story at home; in others they get to discover an epic novel in which the heroes learn the same story as the kids just learnt at church.

When you do this, all of a sudden these handouts become gold to the kids. The kids really want them, and not only do these handouts make it home, they become cherished belongings.

We've also done a series where every handout is part of a bigger poster. The kids can take it home and stick it to their wall and ultimately create a giant image with every piece of the puzzle—which is every handout they get.

These are just a few ways to help the experience kid get a better experience out of the service and then take it back to the community to give them stuff they can only get at church. And let's be honest, this is really fun to do!

See, the church used to be the center of the city in Europe. People always went to the center, where things were happening, and we want to go back to that era, where everything revolves around that community, which is the church. We firmly believe your children's ministry can be that community for the next generation.

NOTES

How this works: Once you find the answers in the chapter, you can note them here for future reference. Also capture your own ideas. You'll often get ideas while reading, which you'll never think of again. So capture them now and implement them over time!

1. Motivation 4 = the e _____ kid
2. Their motivation is: "I want _____
    _____ "
3. Or it is: "I want _____ "
4. Ways to amplify this motivation:

5. Your own ideas to amplify this motivation:

TAKING THINGS FURTHER

TEAM QUESTIONS

Note: The team questions do more than revisit what's taught in the chapter. They help you to take things further than the chapter did. Some things are better discovered by yourself, and as a team. Wouldn't you agree?

1. Do you see a difference between kids who are externally motivated and internally motivated?

2. Do internally motivated kids remain motivated for the long-term? Or are there up and down trends?

3. Have you ever been in a ministry environment where all doors were closed, and you couldn't do what God would have you do? (Think of the town where Jesus "couldn't" do many miracles).

4. Have you spotted any experience kids at your church? What was the experience they came for?

5. What can your ministry do to attract more experience kids?

6. Have you done a children's series that lost momentum over time? And have you done children's series that gained momentum over time?

7. Do you feel that children's ministries rely too much on the parents to bring kids, rather than amplifying kids' own internal motivations to come to church?

8. Pray for the kids out there who go from experience to experience, without knowing that God is their foundation. Pray that they may come to your church to experience life change!

Chapter 6
HOW TO WIN WHEN EVERYBODY ISN'T A WINNER

THE NEXT REASON KIDS come to church might be a surprise: it's competition.

I call this level the competitive kid, and of course, the competitive kid wants to compete. Church can have something for this kid as well. Just think of when the rich young ruler came to Jesus and said, "What do I have to do?" and Jesus gave him a challenge, which was, in a sense, a competition.

It's really great to give kids challenges or something to strive for. We often think, "Oh, they're too young. We should pat them on the back and tell them they're all winners," but in reality, kids love being challenged, they love going for something, they yearn for competition, and if we always have this sort of "everyone's a winner" mentality, then it destroys the motivation for the competitive kid.

SO WHAT MOTIVATES THIS TYPE OF KID?

For this kind of kid, the motivation might be as simple as "I want to win." Sometimes they want to win the prize set out at the end of the competition. Sometimes there's no prize and they just want their team to win.

HOW DO WE AMPLIFY THIS LEVEL OF MOTIVATION?

Amplifying competitive motivation is really fun! You can easily create a series that's full of competition. Right now, we are in the process of creating one where almost every lesson is full of opportunities for kids to compete with each other, so much so that they might even forget they're at church!

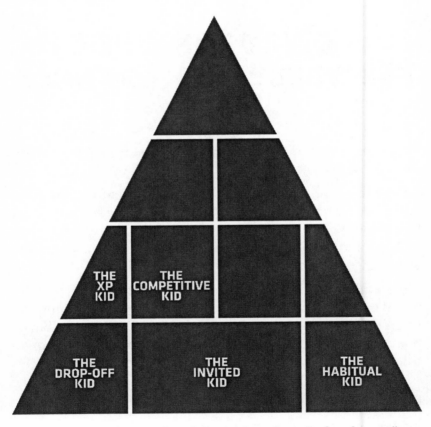

I also know of a youth ministry that does "school wars" every year, where kids from different schools bring their friends and have this beautiful, giant battle with games. It takes place during the service—all the chairs are taken out, and the space becomes a big arena where the kids compete against each other—and then there's 20 minutes of teaching in the middle of the games. It's incredibly popular and goes viral into the community every time it's held. It's really cool.

So you might say, "All right, I want to have this sort of competition, but I can't really change my service at the moment." That's fine. Instead, you might have a dodgeball game *after* the service. That's what we do, and the kids love it. It's a fun sort of community/fellowship thing. We make it at the very end of the service so that kids end up attending both.

Not a fan of dodgeball? Maybe you can have a soccer competition or even something just plain silly. Once we even set up a "chocolate slip and slide," which is basically just a slip and slide with chocolate milk over it. Can you imagine the excitement? The kids compete to see who can slide the farthest across the slip and slide. Any sort of competitive edge will work—just be creative. Add it into your services or right after the service and watch the competitive kids come from every corner of your community.

NOTES

How this works: Once you find the answers in the chapter, you can note them here for future reference. Also capture your own ideas. You'll often get ideas while reading, which you'll never think of again. So capture them now and implement them over time!

1. Motivation 5 = the c _____ kid

2. Their motivation is: "I want _____
   _____ "

3. Ways to amplify this motivation:

4. Your own ideas to amplify this motivation:

TAKING THINGS FURTHER

TEAM QUESTIONS

Note: The team questions do more than revisit what's taught in the chapter. They help you to take things further than the chapter did. Some things are better discovered by yourself, and as a team. Wouldn't you agree?

1. Can you remember not being picked for a game as a kid? Or being picked last? How did that feel? In our lessons we make sure all kids can play each game, every time. Want to guess which type of kid we do that for?

2. Do you have competitive kids in your ministry? How can you have them spread the word to other competitive kids who don't attend your church yet?

3. In the school wars example, you saw how one ministry amplified its competition by adding school pride to the mix. What types of pride exist in your area? Are people proud of their city or neighborhoods? Could you spark a city vs. city competition? Are people proud of their sports, such as their national soccer teams? Could you organize a soccer competition between fans of each team? Or think even edgier: are people proud of their religion? How about a competition between different churches, mosques, temples, in a city-wide peace-making competition organized by your church?

4. Competitions tend to grow when they are repeated. Could you have a yearly competition? A quarterly one? If so, what would it look like? (Note: before you jump in, try it once, and then scale it up if it works. Only continue an effort when it builds momentum.)

5. Take a look at your current curriculum. How can you add competition elements? (Example: after each segment, have a kid from the team who won that segment do the next move in a game. For instance, they could add a disk at Four in a Row, or they could add their team's symbol in Tic-Tac-Toe.) Also be careful not to add competition all the time. Balance it. Some series have more competition than others. Variety is key.

6. Which of the volunteers are competitive? How could their competitiveness be utilized? Could they become team captains? Dress up in the team's colors? Should more than one person emcee a service, like all the team champions at once?

7. This chapter showed that prizes are useful, but it's good for them to eventually disappear. Do you agree? How does your ministry use prizes well? What would your ministry look like when prizes are phased out? Would the competitive kid love the competition without needing a prize at the end?

8. Pray for your community, and for the thousands of people who flock to the sports parks each week. Pray they'll find their way to church, and that God will help you find your way to them.

Chapter 7
AN ARMY OF SOCIAL BUTTERFLIES

THE NEXT TYPE OF COMMITMENT we find in our triangle is a social commitment. We find this kind of commitment with the social kid.

The social kid's motivation for coming to church is, "I want to see my friends and my leader." This is a bit of a higher motivation because it's not just about the fun, games, and stories; it's starting to become more about the people. And that's really good! It's getting us closer to what church is all about.

The social kid really wants to be loved or wants to love others. Or maybe they're just a social butterfly. Or all these things are combined in a social kid.

AMPLIFYING THIS LEVEL OF MOTIVATION

A way to amplify this type of motivation is to use connectors, which is the name we give to volunteers whose main task is to interact with kids (we also refer to them as roamers, because they are given few tasks other than roaming around, finding unplanned ways to serve through relationships).

Developing connectors and roamers is amazing work. It's more complicated than just throwing some volunteers into a room and saying, "Go connect with the kids—good luck!" Does your ministry have volunteers standing in the back? Each ministry sees this phenomenon. You can remove this problem by giving your volunteers access to training on what to do when the service is going on. In other words, train them to be roamers and connectors.

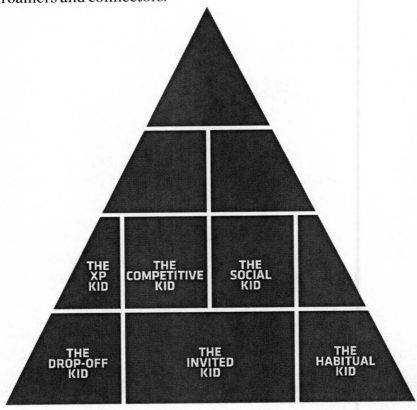

Together with your volunteers, decide on some challenges for them. Give them five or six things to teach kids. Or teach them ways to have spiritual conversations with children. In every ministry I've served in, the connectors and roamers are given explicit encouragement to walk around and talk with kids *while* the service is in session—and generally the ministry results will double. The stories that come out of their interactions are just incredible.

Connectors and roamers are also given the authority to take kids to the hallway or any open space in order to have private conversations with them. This could be with kids individually or with a group. Sometimes when conversations are about deep things, kids can let their tears flow, so it's really important that these connectors and roamers establish great relationships with these kids.

50 PERCENT MORE EFFECT

In our philosophy, we say 50 percent of the ministry is done through the program, and the other 50 percent through the connectors and their relationships with the kids. If you only have a program, then that's your 100 percent. You can double that by training up connectors! Connectors work with the program, but have goals of their own as they lead and follow up with kids from week to week. In order to help them see that their ministry is independent from the program, we joke that for them, the program is just an excuse for kids to be there so that relationships can be made!

Personally, I love being a connector or a roamer more than leading the ministry or being on stage. As a connector, you really get to have friendships and relationships with the kids, sometimes to the point where you'll visit them in the hospital or go to their soccer games or form small groups with them.

God-willing, we hope to write another book on all the different things roamers and connectors can teach the kids, how they track kids' spiritual progress, the five methods they use to lead kids to Christ, how they give new kids a full overview of the Bible in less than five minutes, and many of the other things we've developed. But for now, you have a good idea on what roamers are and what they can mean to your ministry.

AMPLIFYING THIS LEVEL OF MOTIVATION

The social kids come for the connections, and there's no better way to foster connections than having connectors. They make sure no kid is ever alone, feels out of place, or doesn't feel valued.

Another way to amplify this commitment is to have fun little games before or after the service to encourage families to keep hanging out on the patio or garden or wherever there is space for people to mingle. Children's ministries are sometimes so prison-like: "Check in, check out...walk through this line...sit in these chairs." If you have areas where people can hang out after checkout, it can be a lot of fun and can help build some really strong relationships between the kids and between both kids and leaders. So perhaps you could have a plaza with games (if you need some game suggestions, try "Nine in the Sky" or "Gaga Ball"; they're quite inexpensive games to set up and give hours of fun). You could even have free food or drinks after the service. Encourage that family vibe. You can possibly even create a team that works together with multiple ministries just for social activities like this. It's your prerogative.

The last way to foster connections is to have small groups. It doesn't matter whether you have small groups as part of the weekend service or as a separate discipleship program. Small groups make a large church feel smaller. But make sure that connections are actually fostered, and it's not just a chance to work through curriculum.

NOTES

How this works: Once you find the answers in the chapter, you can note them here for future reference. Also capture your own ideas. You'll often get ideas while reading, which you'll never think of again. So capture them now and implement them over time!

1. Motivation 6 = the s_____ kid
2. Their motivation is: "I want to_____
   _____."
3. Ways to amplify this motivation:

4. Your own ideas to amplify this motivation:

TAKING THINGS FURTHER

TEAM QUESTIONS

Note: The team questions do more than revisit what's taught in the chapter. They help you to take things further than the chapter did. Some things are better discovered by yourself, and as a team. Wouldn't you agree?

1. Which of your volunteers used to be—or currently are—social butterflies?

2. Let's dream. What would your ministry look like if it was *the* place for people to casually hang and connect? Could this happen with your children's ministry?

3. Have you ever had kids sitting alone at church? If so, do you know why?

4. You saw multiple ways to invite kids to join your group. Which of the ways fits you best? What invitations do you use?

5. Are your ministry's volunteers allowed to "work the room" while the service is going on? If they are, it does add a bit of controlled chaos. Would your ministry be able to handle this? If not, how could you get to that point?

6. Which kids do you wish you had more time with? Which ones are still "closed mysteries"? If you knew you couldn't fail, how would you serve them? What would you talk about?

7. Connectors (or roamers) are a completely different "branch" of your children's ministry as those who set up and run the program. However, at times it's good to let connectors do something on stage as well, so that they're put in the spotlight for the kids. This helps them create connections better. Knowing this, how would you

structure your team of connectors? Maybe have them do one thing on stage, and connect during the other times? How would you schedule it?

8. Pray for the kids whose stories have come out in your ministry. Pray for the kids whose stories you don't yet know. Pray for the kids who don't yet attend your church, but who desperately look for connections.

Chapter 8
BECOMING THE BUZZ OF THE COMMUNITY

SO FAR WE HAVE THE drop-off kid, the invited kid, and the habitual kid on the bottom of our triangle. The next level gives us the experience kid, the competitive kid, the social kid, and, finally, the buzz kid.

The buzz kid—no, not the haircut—is basically the kid who goes to church because of the buzz in the community. Whatever's trendy is what they go for. Usually these are the popular kids or the ones who follow whatever's cool in the moment so that they, too, can increase their cool.

Their motivation is, "I want to hear what everybody is talking about." Maybe your ministry has been the buzz of the community before, or maybe it will be. Implementing what we've laid out will certainly help. Once your ministry is "buzzing," the buzz kid wants to be a part of it.

I know, this whole idea about a "buzz" feels weird. But in the Bible, God spread his fame with wave after wave. He let his people go through the sea, just so the surrounding nations would take notice. And when Jesus was on earth, we constantly read that "the news spread through the region." Jesus' ministry had more than a buzz. He sent out shockwaves that changed the fabric of time. Jesus constantly spoke of the kingdom of God. That was his main message. He spoke of God's kingdom arriving, and wherever he arrived, the kingdom of God was there. And whenever the kingdom of God arrives, things shake up. Earth and its inhabitants are being restored to their original intent. Lives are put together again. People are made whole. We see a glimpse of what Eden was like and what heaven will be like. So let's not say that it's not humble to have your ministry be the buzz of the community. It's not us doing it. It's God spreading the word through you.

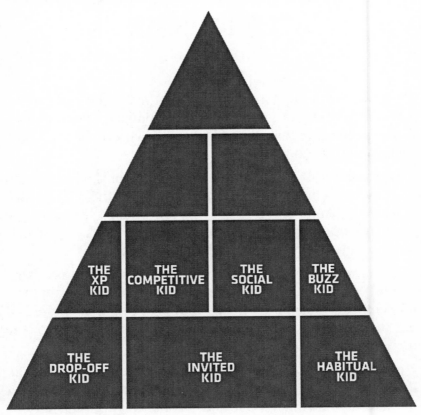

AMPLIFYING THIS LEVEL OF MOTIVATION

One way to amplify this type of motivation—and to reach this type of kid, since you don't have direct access to them—is to distribute "spreadables" to the kids already in the ministry.

Spreadables are visible things that enter the kids' world and start conversations about your church. For instance, you can give your kids armbands or even T-shirts with the name of your church on them. I'm involved in one youth ministry that distributes these awesome T-shirts (that are also really comfortable) and challenges the kids to have a day where they all wear their T-shirts to school, kind of like an "on-Tuesdays-we-wear-our-church-shirts" kind of thing. The funny thing is that these shirts don't even have the name of the youth ministry on them. It's just the abbreviation. Three letters, that's it. But it starts conversations because their peers ask them what the three letters mean.

Sometimes the kids from the ministry even self-organize, which is really cool, and they start posting things on Instagram and Facebook. Everybody ends up asking, "What's this shirt for?!" or "What are you guys doing?!" and it goes viral. So be creative, be edgy, but also make sure to do everyone else and yourself a favor to get some high-quality shirts because you want kids to hang on to them.

A more inexpensive way to create spreadables is to have your connectors and roamers make drawings for the kids as they're walking around the service talking to them. Fun drawings always make it home. I once drew a doodle as I sat in church and the kid next to me wanted to have it. It spread like wildfire through the row and the other kids wanted one as well. So while the service was going on, I kept doodling. It quickly became a weekly thing where kids were eager to get something as simple as a doodle.

I once ran out of paper but this kid really wanted a drawing, so I drew a little picture on his hand. It was a silly little fish or something, and the kid loved it so much that he traced it throughout the week so he wouldn't lose it. And then, when he went to school, the other kids saw it and said, "Oh, look at that funny drawing! Where did you get that?" and—boom—that's the ministry spilling out even more into the community. All the kid had to say was, "At church." Two words, and the news spread.

A kid named Carson brought three new kids, who wanted to come simply to "meet the person who makes the drawings at Carson's church." And that's the power of a roamer. Many more kids have come for the drawings and many family cousins and nephews and neighbors have come simply to get a drawing, and then fell in love with the church.

So if your roamers have drawing skills, have them draw little doodles or caricatures. We actually hardly draw on paper anymore. It's much better to draw on kids' hands because they literally become a walking billboard! We do always ask first, "Would your parents be okay with a drawing on your hand?" 99.99 percent of the time, the answer is yes. Over many years we've only had one angry parent because they were going to a wedding after, which the kid forgot about. But this percentage is so low that it's not a problem at all.

As you see, spreadables don't have to be expensive. They can be practically free.

THE WONDERS OF TECHNOLOGY

Another important thing—and I really want to stress this—is to let kids use their phones.

In children's ministry we often tell kids, "Put your phones away! Put your phones away!" but what if we did the opposite?

Imagine having an emcee at your children's or youth ministry who's really funny, and a kid wants to film it with his phone. I've seen this so many times. Instead of stopping them, let them take the video so they can show their friends and spread the love. It's totally fine. When we did those teaching series with the stories that I told you about, there were some kids who wanted to see the story again, so they basically filmed the entire thing (and sometimes they would be about 15 minutes long!) so they could watch it again later. This type of thing is excellent. Some of them had friends of another religion, who would never attend church. They still wanted to show the story to them. Let them!

Smartphones are actually by far the number one spreadable—more so even than T-shirts and bracelets. Remember those handouts I mentioned earlier? The ones with the videogame codes? Well, we also put social media challenges on those handouts. This way, they spread what they've learnt on Instagram or Snapchat or whatever they're on nowadays. You may be thinking, "What? For children's ministry?!" Absolutely! Seven- and eight-year-olds have phones now because parents see it as a safety thing. And they use social media too. It's part of their culture, so let them do their thing.

Let's be honest, if you were a kid who does not attend church, would you want to be invited through a polished invite-card, or would you want your friend to show you the funny things that happen at his awesome church?

EXTRA:

While writing this chapter, I received a message from a kid we served in Norway. His message came out of the blue and made me deeply grateful for what God does when you serve others. The kid said, "Dude we miss you guys so much, we NEED to meet again! I was so calm when I was with you, as if we had met many times before. I am proud to call you and your brother friends."

I never knew God used us to have this "calming" effect. He was one of the kids who didn't say much when we were there. It goes to show that if you're a roamer or connector, you have no idea what God does through you. You may feel that "ministry didn't go well this week," but you don't get to decide that! God decides how well it went, because he did the work, and his work is often invisible. He does things through you and me that we have no knowledge of.

The second thing this message shows is that when you're a roamer inside the walls of the church, you can also be one outside the walls of the church as well, in this case, all the way in Norway! Let God use you to serve kids everywhere. Your church is only a training ground for a lifelong ministry!

NOTES

How this works: Once you find the answers in the chapter, you can note them here for future reference. Also capture your own ideas. You'll often get ideas while reading, which you'll never think of again. So capture them now and implement them over time!

1. Motivation 7 = the b_____ kid

2. Their motivation is: "I want to_____
   _____."

3. Ways to amplify this motivation:

4. Your own ideas to amplify this motivation:

TAKING THINGS FURTHER

TEAM QUESTIONS

Note: The team questions do more than revisit what's taught in the chapter. They help you to take things further than the chapter did. Some things are better discovered by yourself, and as a team. Wouldn't you agree?

1. Has your children's ministry ever become the buzz of the community? If not, what could this look like? Feel free to dream!

2. Do you feel it's prideful to want the news of your ministry to spread, or do you feel it's exactly what should happen? What happened with Jesus' ministry?

3. We looked at multiple spreadables, from armbands to shirts to handouts. What spreadables could work for you?

4. One spreadable is free and comes out of the friendships between your leaders and the kids: fun little drawings. What little doodles can you make?

5. The spreadable of little drawings was discovered by accident. It began simply by hanging out with the kids. Are volunteers in your ministry free to make up fun little things? Are there times when they're too restricted by the policies, rules, regulations, and expectations? What could your ministry do to foster relationships by taking the lid off?

6. Have your kids been able to spread the word about your ministry by using their phones? How have they done so? How could they do so in the future?

7. Could you add fun segments in your program and allow (or encourage) kids to film it? (It could be as simple as having a leader put a pie in the face of another leader).

8. Ask God to go before you and spread his word. Ask him how we—his servants—could not stand in his way, but join where he is going. Ask him to give you his ideas on how to spread the word.

Chapter 9

THE EFFECT OF DELIGHTFUL TEACHING

BEFORE TELLING YOU THE next motivation, we need to clear up a huge misunderstanding in today's Christianity. This misunderstanding mostly reigns throughout the United States, but it's also present among Christians in other nations. In a sense, this misunderstanding is always present in some form. Let's take a look at what it is, starting off with a tiny little verse.

The book of Ecclesiastes hurls a surprisingly fun verse into our lives: "The Preacher sought to find delightful words and to write words of truth correctly" (12:10). Another translation says, "The spokesman tried to find just the right words. He wrote the words of truth very carefully." It shows how a good preacher seeks to delight his audience, by preaching the truth in a delightful way. This doesn't mean the Preacher watered down the message. He still preached the unchanging truth, but he did it in a delightful way.

In today's Christianity we often have the idea that the truth has to hurt, and if it doesn't, it's not truth. For a few years now, I've heard Christians aggress against being "politically correct." The idea is that it's better to speak one's mind than to be oppressed and squashed into political correctness. But when the proponent of this idea then speaks his mind, it's often done in a harsh and uninviting way. The result isn't too rosy. The message doesn't come across at all. All people see is intolerance, anger, and no willingness to listen. People don't accept our message because we don't have enough love to say it in a way that they can understand. We don't say it in their words. And so they turn away from us. And what do we do in response? We just say that they're ignoring God's word. We then go on saying that they can only be changed if we throw more truth at them, in the same harsh and inconsiderate way.

We've got it all wrong.

What we're trying to do here is not wise. It's foolish. The Bible says that the Preacher was wise and he "sought to find delightful words and to write the words of truth correctly."

When we read that line carefully, we see that there's two parts to that verse. One is to find delightful words; the other is to write the truth correctly. The two belong to each other. No, we don't have to hide the truth. We don't have to be hushed by society. And if we define "political correctness" as "hiding our faith and values," then no, we don't need to be that version of politically correct. But we do need to speak the truth in love, and love means finding words people will understand. Or better, find words that delight our audience.

We like to say, "I'm not politically correct, I'm just correct." But either option is an extreme. The Bible proposes a third option: what if we are delightfully correct?

Think about it. Delightfully correct. It means you're correct (the truth doesn't change), but you're also delightful to your audience. How? Because you—just like the Preacher—sought to find delightful words. By being delightfully correct, you're no longer a doormat (politically correct), and you're no longer a brick wall (harshly correct). Instead, you're an open door. You are inviting people into the truth.

Look at what the Preacher did. He sought delightful words. The King James Version says he "sought to find acceptable words." Acceptable. That's neither harsh nor compromised. It's acceptable to both sides of the argument. Acceptable means "words the audience delights in" and it also means "words you find acceptable." Acceptable words are a bridge between those who believe and those who don't. And trust me, the Bible has so much truth, that even those who disagree with God's word will find biblical truths they delight in. I firmly believe that every truth from the Bible can be said in a way that both sides agree with. We just have to find the right words, the keys to their hearts. And God guides us in that endeavor. After all, isn't Jesus called "the word of God"? That's how important words are.

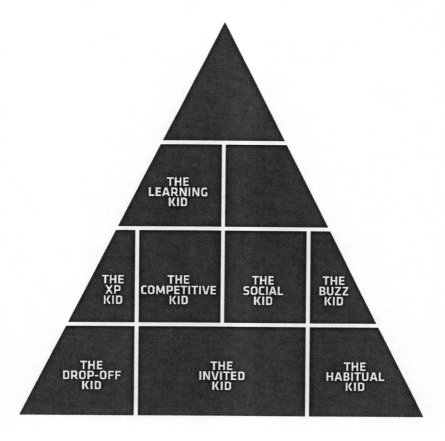

Here's the real problem: we simply assume that people don't want to hear the truth. We've already decided that they will say "no" to the truth. And that's why we don't bother to find delightful words. And in doing so, we are missing out on so much blessing, on so much delight, on seeing so much life-change! Because when God has us delight others with his delightful words, he has us delight in that delight as well.

We had to clear this up because delightful teaching is the reason the next type of kid comes to church. We call this kid the learning kid. And the learning kid is interested in today's subject.

Now hold up. Wait a minute. We rarely see kids who are delighted to learn today's subject. Why is that? Because we don't tell them in advance what today's subject is going to be. But when we do—everything changes for the learning kid.

SO WHAT MOTIVATES THIS TYPE OF KID?

The learning kids come to church because they truly desire to possess the knowledge of whatever subject you're covering that day. Their motivation is, "I really want to know this."

Don't you want every kid to be like that?

We grossly underestimate this kind of motivation in children's ministry. Since we don't often advertise or tell kids in advance what they'll be learning in church, how can they be excited about it if they don't know what it's going to be about?

In youth ministry, we usually tell kids what they can expect and often adults too, but kids just have to show up and see what happens—kind of like school. Come on, guys, we really don't want to be like school! Luckily, there are many delightful ways to let kids know what you've got for them. I'm delighted to tell you how we've done it, and I'd love to hear what you'll come up with. (Note that I used the word "delighted" in the last two sentences. Coincidence? I think not!)

AMPLIFYING THIS LEVEL OF MOTIVATION

We can make our services irresistible to the learning kid by advertising the subjects to kids in advance. This gives them a chance to anticipate what subjects they'll be exploring, and it also gives you a chance to frame subjects in a way that is inviting. It's very important to show the themes in a way that's incredibly inviting. That's where the "delightful words" part comes in. The beautiful thing is that it doesn't matter what curriculum you're using or what you're teaching on—you can always find a way to present the upcoming subjects in an inviting way.

Let's look at some examples:

In our David series, we had certain lesson goals. The goal of the first lesson is to teach kids to set their hearts on God, just as David set his heart on God. But most kids, even the ones highly motivated by learning, might not be particularly excited to learn about "setting your heart on God," especially when it is worded in this way. But if you frame it a little differently, in a way that is more exciting to children, then you can enhance their willingness to hear the lesson.

So what did we come up with? Well, this series of David was all about David's leadership qualities, so we rephrased the subject as, "The Number One Secret of a Great Leader." As kids go through the lesson, they'll learn that "setting your heart on God" *is* "the number one secret of a great leader." See how this leadership twist is a much more hospitable introduction? It's a great way to help kids get excited to learn about the important information within the lesson in the first place.

The whole series on David is about leadership, so we turned every title to that. The next week of the David series had us teach on "obey even if you don't understand." Now, is that an engaging title? No. Is it a biblical truth that needs to be taught? Absolutely. Do kids need to know that they need to obey God even when they don't understand? Absolutely. Sometimes they need to obey their parents too even when they don't understand, right? So, yes, it's a really good thing to learn, but it's just not a very engaging title. A better title might be "The One Thing Every Great Leader Knows." And then throughout the lesson, kids will find out that every great leader knows that they should obey God even if they don't understand.

See the progression from one week to the next? First "The Number One Secret of a Great Leader" (set your heart on God), then "The One Thing Every Great Leader Knows" (obey even if you don't understand), and then "What a Great Leader Believes" (what we're actually teaching here is the belief that God will save you—it's a salvation week).

Go over all the subjects that you're going to teach on, and see how you can speak the kids' language of what you're teaching. The rule of thumb is: Start with what kids care about, then teach them what they should care about, and eventually they'll care about that as well. You start where they are, not where you want them to be.

Some more examples:

WHAT YOU'RE TEACHING	HOW YOU TITLE IT
God loves you	Discover the person who loves you more than your parents do
Read the Bible daily	How to be refreshed each day
Love your neighbor	How to become a person most people like
How to deal with anger	The secret to controlling yourself when you're super angry

THE EFFECT OF THE LEARNING KID

The learning kid has a powerful influence on the rest of the room, often without realizing it. Even if there are only a few kids who are interested in learning, they'll raise the interest level of the entire room of kids. Their interest in the subject is almost contagious, and you really want to capitalize on that because you want the teaching to be the most interesting thing about coming to church, more than the games and prizes.

What we've done is create teaching series based on the things kids really want to learn from the Bible. This is specifically focused on the learning kid, and also on developing more learning kids. We gathered kids' toughest questions—especially the ones that children's ministries rarely teach on—and answer those in the series. But before we wrote the series, we first user-tested the answers with them. We wanted to be sure that these answers came across as best as they could. This process took us five years. We called the series, "Life's Biggest Questions," and every week we have a different question that kids have asked us.

To give you an example, the first week in the series of "Life's Biggest Questions" is "How Do I Know if God Is Real?" That's a deep question! And how *do* you know if God is real? That's hard to teach unless you have a good curriculum to help you teach it. Once you do, it's actually quite easy. Once you tell kids that you're teaching on the subject, you'll see them go, "I've always sort of wanted to know that, but I didn't dare ask it out loud." It's a wonderful thing. By teaching the answers to their deepest questions, you're waking up more questions inside of them, and they begin to dare to ask more. And that's what you want!

In some religions, kids aren't allowed to ask questions. Not so in Christianity! The more they can ask, the better!

Then the next week we'd ask, "So if God Is Real, Why Is He Invisible?" Well, the Bible gives us three answers for that, which can then turn into a practical friendship with God. Kids want to know these things.

This previous question leads right into next week's question, which is "Where Did God Come From?" That's a huge one! You would not believe the number of kids who think that God is an alien who came from an alien spaceship. I know it sounds crazy, but kids see these things in movies, and it kind of trickles into their consciousness because the church doesn't offer an alternative.

If you lead your series with these kinds of questions or you can develop your curriculum in a way that addresses these things, it can really raise the interest level of these kids, and you basically end up with a lot more kids who have now become "the learning kid."

THE BIBLICAL EXAMPLE OF THE LEARNING KID

The biblical example of the learning kid is, of course, Jesus himself. He spent three days at the temple without his parents. A question I often ask myself is, "If my church was open 24/7, would these kids come to church and be there for three days just like Jesus was—just so they could constantly learn?

I was volunteering at a Christian camp a couple years back and I was given a group of kids for five days. I didn't feel the camp curriculum challenged the kids enough, so I started asking my group deep questions. It's funny what happens when you do so. When you start asking kids deep questions, deep questions come back to you. It's the best way to have them start thinking. Kids tend to start opening up to the questions they have in their hearts and begin to realize how many questions they actually have.

During the last two days of camp, there was a five-hour block where the kids could do anything they wanted—paintball, BB guns, archery, soccer, basketball competitions, you name it—and yet the group of kids I was with decided to stay with me for the entire block, five full hours, asking questions about God!

Can you imagine kids sitting for five hours? I certainly can't. And can you imagine kids sitting for five hours while they could be playing paintball? While others kids come by yelling how awesome they were at soccer? But these kids didn't leave. They stayed under the massive tree we were sitting under. It felt like the time of the New Testament! All they wanted was to ask more and more questions. The conversations got so deep that kids were crying and sayings things like, "I always wanted to know the answers to these questions!"

Why did this happen on the last day of camp? It's because during the week I had constantly been asking kids about these profound things, and now they were reciprocating. It was about fostering this culture of "the learning kid." They had all become "the learning kid."

WHEN KIDS DON'T ASK MANY QUESTIONS

One more thing needs to be said. Have you ever said, "Hey kids, if you have any questions, come to any of the leaders! We're here for you!"

I've said this many times, and I have to admit, it hardly ever works. I never figured out why it doesn't work, until I found out what does. In the camp example above, you saw what does work. When you start asking questions, they begin asking back. Once you're versatile at this method, you open the gospels and you just smile when you see Jesus doing the same. Jesus asked his disciples, "Who do the people say I am?" And then he followed up with the kicker, "And who do you think I am?" He constantly dropped question-bombs like that.

So why does it not work to just tell kids to come to you? Because you haven't established a question-based relationship. Instead of establishing a question-based relationship, you were on stage. You were teaching. But everything changes when you hang out with kids and drop a question-bomb Jesus-style. You don't even have to give the answer. It's better not to. Just leave them with an unsolved mystery and let it grow in their hearts. They'll be back, oh they'll be back! If you're not careful, they'll be five-hours-back! (Or they'll be three-days back if they're 12-year-old Jesus, ha!).

You can do this from stage as well, by the way. Drop a question-bomb and don't give the answer yet. Tell them to think about it throughout the week. Then the next week, ask the question again, and don't give the answer. Those who are ready to learn will come up to you to ask the answer. Well done, you just found the learning kids!

The more you do this, the more question-based relationships you'll foster, and kids will start to ask more and more questions. It starts slowly and then turns into an avalanche. You'll see questions basically exploding from these kids' hearts. They'll finally feel like they're learning things at church because they're coming with their *own* questions instead of just waiting for your curriculum to decide what you're going to teach them.

When you see this happening, it kind of makes your jaw drop: "Wow, I've been in ministry so long, and I actually stopped believing that kids want to hear about Christ." When you see kids' tears flow because the lies of cultures are shed, and the truth of Christ fills their hearts, you won't be able to keep your eyes dry yourself. (In Chapter 11 you'll read more about unleashing this question-volley-phenomenon and how to foster it, and the series "Life's Biggest Questions" has an even more practical step-by-step guide on reaching this level in your ministry throughout the series).

There are tons of kids with external motivations, but once the learning kid emerges and explodes through the ministry, you will see a surge of interest toward Christ. It just rejuvenates your heart as a minister because that's why you joined the ministry in the first place.

I want that for you and your ministry so badly.

NOTES

How this works: Once you find the answers in the chapter, you can note them here for future reference. Also capture your own ideas. You'll often get ideas while reading, which you'll never think of again. So capture them now and implement them over time!

1.   Motivation 8 = the l_____ kid

2.   Their motivation is: "I really _____
_____ "

3.   Ways to amplify this motivation:

4.   Your own ideas to amplify this motivation:

TAKING THINGS FURTHER

TEAM QUESTIONS

Note: The team questions do more than revisit what's taught in the chapter. They help you to take things further than the chapter did. Some things are better discovered by yourself, and as a team. Wouldn't you agree?

1. Have you felt the tension between telling the truth and telling the truth in love?

2. Have you ever been on stage and searched for delightful words, but you had a brain freeze? Or have you walked away and then thought, "Oh boy, that's how I should have said it!" (Don't worry, we all have!)

3. How can you teach in such a way that it appeals to the learning kid and brings out their passion to learn? Could you delay answers? Could you advertise the teaching themes in advance?

4. Take your current teaching series and write the themes out in an inviting way. Then user-test these themes with kids and see which themes make their eyes light up.

5. I've been in meetings where well-intended children's ministers tried to understand kids indirectly. For instance, they'd want kids to make drawings and then see what their drawings would say about the kids. There's a much easier way to get to know what kids want—ask them! What's something you should be asking your kids?

6. Whenever you're interacting with kids, what questions could you ask—without giving the answer—in order to foster a culture where questions can freely pop up?

7. Have you seen the learning kid break through the crowd, changing the mood in the room? It could be when they

ask a great question, or when they tell other kids to be quiet because they "really want to learn this." Does your curriculum help the learning kid come out of the woodwork? Does it foster a hunger for Christ in kids, or does it more or less dump teaching on them without regarding what kids are interested in?

8. Pray that God will give the kids a huge hunger for his word, a hunger like that of the psalmist in Psalm 119.

Chapter 10

KIDS WHO LIKE ACTIONS MORE THAN WORDS

WHEN YOU'RE TEACHING, you don't want kids to just soak up the words and think about them. You don't even want them to merely believe it. You want them to put those words into action. To put God's word into action. That is obedience, and anything less than that is just that—it's less than that!

Luckily, some kids seem to naturally be more inclined to actions than words. These kids are ready to serve. We call these the serving kids. (Points for original naming, right?) Some kids have the gift of serving and helping out feels natural to them. But even kids who don't have that gift love helping out. Kids love to be part of shaping something that has meaning.

A lesson can be learnt from the games industry. Back in the day, games used to be made *for* the kids, not *with* the kids, but the industry discovered that kids want to influence the game itself. They want to shape their own character, build their own worlds, use their own creativity. So customization was introduced and this was wildly popular. Then it grew from customization to completely customizable game-forms where the player decides almost everything. A current example of that is Minecraft—arguably the most popular game for kids ever.

Think about importing that principle into your children's ministry. What would happen if you gave up some control, and had kids take ownership of it? You could start the same way as the games industry, with some customization, and end up with a ministry where kids influence nearly every facet of the ministry. Your ministry's style may no longer feel as slick and professional as a highly produced Disney-show, but your ministry would be *theirs*. And that's far more valuable.

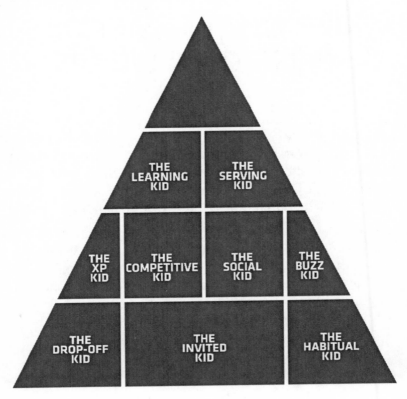

SO WHAT MOTIVATES THE SERVING KID?

The serving kid loves to serve—and there are many of them. They come to make a difference. Their motivation is "I'm helping out." Check out the story below.

•••

NATHAN'S BAFFLING STORY

Nathan was just the sweetest and most innocent third-grader. He always came to church wanting to help in any way he could. Every week he would say, "Is there anything I can help with?" He had this extreme gift of service. He didn't want to help just to skip the service, or to have a position other kids wouldn't have. Nathan truly wanted to serve. He wanted to be part of the team and didn't see his young age as an obstacle to that. Neither did we.

The first couple of weeks, of course, there was very little he could actually help with, but finally I just went room to room looking at all the different aspects in the ministry to find something he could help with.

We had an amazing third grade leader named Stacey, and she said, "You know what...I got this," and she found places where Nathan could help out, even with things that could be considered a little beyond his age, such as helping with the sound system. But little Nathan did great.

Stacey just let him serve because he was just so great at serving. At one point, though, God called Stacey away from our ministry to another ministry, and the leader who replaced her just didn't have the same ability to find places where Nathan could do his thing. She enforced the age policies and Nathan found himself out of a role to serve.

He kept asking and asking, but eventually he stopped coming to church. All he wanted was to be a part of something, to serve the church in whatever way he could, and it was a very sad realization for us that he stopped coming because his commitment was not being reciprocated by the church.

Nathan is a teenager now and he found our Instagram account two months ago. We were overjoyed to be in touch again. He joined us when we took a group of teenagers to the movies.

At the theatre, we recorded a video for Stacey and sent it over. He remembered her after all these years. It was an awesome digital re-connect.

Nathan now helps his father do audio at church services.

AMPLIFYING THIS LEVEL OF MOTIVATION

It's easy to motivate the serving kid: have places to serve!

Look at your curriculum, at every segment you do, and think, "What responsibilities can we give away to the kids?"

I once talked with a lady who leads a mind-blowing children's ministry in Germany, and she said, "Kids who serve are kids who stay," and she was right. Nathan's story proves it.

We often think that kids need to be attending church for a while before they're ready to serve, but this isn't always true. Sometimes, kids who just started coming are already ready to serve. We once met twin kids at the movie theatre. They recognized us from Instagram and they were overjoyed to meet us, since we're twins as well. We wasted no time and invited them to church. But week after week, they couldn't make it. Finally, they could make it to church on a Saturday evening, the exact evening when we had to DJ at the youth ministry. We had an important program to pull off, and we knew we'd be too busy to receive new kids. And that's a problem because we should never be too busy to receive new kids. So we asked them if they wanted to come an hour early to help us set up the event. They'd help build the DJ booth, and even be part of the program by having the smoke machines go off on time, help us into the robot suits, and more. The twins were overjoyed to help us out. They got to be backstage the first time they attended church! The event was a massive success and one of the twins became a regular attender. Not just him, but his group of friends as well. (By the way, you can watch a recording of the DJ event on our YouTube channel. Search for "Tornado Twins Live Performance Glow Party." It might just give you some fun, creative ideas on how to lead a crowd without saying a word on stage!)

We advise you to have kids serve as soon as possible. It's best to start them off serving. Why teach kids to serve later? When you start them off serving, you set a precedent. When serving is in their inception of church-attendance, then they're most likely to continue a serving attitude throughout their lives.

The thing that holds us back is our own thinking. We've come to believe that the only way to serve is in an official capacity. And once we have kids serve in official capacities, the ministry depends on them. And then it's really scary when they don't show up.

But there's more ways to serve than serving in an official capacity. In the DJ example, the twins could come and serve just that one time and it was perfect. The ministry didn't break if they didn't attend the next week. We can find many more "nonessential serving opportunities" like that. In our other book, *Kidmin Reformation,* we give you step by step ways to have kids serve. We also describe how you won't waste your time with extra meetings and rehearsals and all those things that make it hard on you to have kids serve.

AN EASY WAY TO HAVE KIDS BE THE TEACHERS

If your curriculum has long segments, it's hard to have kids teach. In the curriculum we write, we purposefully keep each segment short. We'd rather have more short segments than fewer long. We jokingly call this the shotgun approach. The segments rapid-fire, keeping the service nice and fast for this ADD generation.

When the segments are short, you can go ahead and give some away to the kids. Sometimes they're *so* easy, in fact, that ten minutes before the service, you can say to a kid, "Hey, do you want to do something on stage?" and with a couple of lines of explanation as to what you want, they can do it.

If you're thinking, "Well, no, the kids in my ministry need more preparation than that," then you might be right. But if you change the curriculum to make things simpler, then kids can take it on from time to time. Once you dial the knobs a little and tweak things, you'll find all sorts of fun ways for kids to do all sorts of awesome stuff, and that's just another explosion in your ministry. An explosion of serving kids.

TRANSFORMING YOUR MINISTRY

When you extrapolate this principle, you can have kids play in the band, be the worship leaders, do motions, do light and sound, be roamers and connectors, be emcees who lead games and other segments, and even do the call for their peers to accept Christ.

I believe that kids want to be picked to serve almost as much as they want to be picked for a game, especially if it's something fun. So do it. Unleash the serving kids, and more serving kids will come. If you're ever low on volunteers, look no further. You already have them in your room—they're just a little younger than expected.

NOTES

How this works: Once you find the answers in the chapter, you can note them here for future reference. Also capture your own ideas. You'll often get ideas while reading, which you'll never think of again. So capture them now and implement them over time!

1. Motivation 9 = the s_____ kid
2. Their motivation is: "I'm _____"

3. Ways to amplify this motivation:

4. Your own ideas to amplify this motivation:

TAKING THINGS FURTHER

TEAM QUESTIONS

Note: The team questions do more than revisit what's taught in the chapter. They help you to take things further than the chapter did. Some things are better discovered by yourself, and as a team. Wouldn't you agree?

1. Identify some of the serving kids in your ministry.

2. Have you desired to see kids serve more, but ran into the fact that they can be unreliable in attendance or their commitment?

3. What are ways you can have kids serve without the ministry breaking when kids don't show or don't follow through?

4. What's a way you can have new kids serve right away?

5. Let's dream. What would a children's ministry look like if all the adults did was teach the children how to run the ministry themselves? Would it be possible?

6. I know a youth ministry that, once a year, has a series where the kids lead the services. It's done by school. So one week, the kids from one school "own the weekend." The next week the kids from the next school "own the weekend." How could you implement (parts of) this idea into your children's ministry?

7. Can you give some of the teaching away to kids? (Note: if you have wireless mics, you can just keep your own mic and give the kids another. If order needs to return to the room, you can simply "pause" the kid who is presenting, and quickly bring order to the room, and then let the kid continue.)

8. Pray that God will give your kids a deep desire to serve him, and that they'll discover some of the giftedness that he has given them. Pray that more kids will get to serve in your ministry, and that this will be the beginning of a life of service for them! (Note: many of those who have done children's ministry for over 10 years started in their youth! After doing a survey on this, I'd say it's easily over 50 percent. How many lifelong children's ministers will you raise up?)

Chapter 11
THE KIDS WHO FOUND OUT WHAT IT'S ALL ABOUT

SINCE YOU READ THIS FAR, I'm going to reward you with some extra tips and tricks, which I packed into this chapter. It has more insights than the other chapters have.

You've reached that chapter that reveals the highest level of motivation, and that is the kid who has a deep hunger for God. It's that kid who knows he wants to get closer to his Creator. It's the kid who is the same way Jesus was at 12, when he said, "Didn't you know I had to be in my Father's house?"

Boy, those words.

They get me every time.

Didn't you know I had to be in my Father's house?

Didn't you know, Mom? Dad? Why did you search for me? Didn't you know?

We have such an awesome responsibility that we get to orchestrate and organize their Father's house. That this can be the place they run to. That this can be the place that helps them to get closer to their number one friend—their Maker.

We call this kid "the godly kid" because they want God. That's what they come for. That's *who* they come for.

And boy, don't you wish all kids had this level of motivation?

SO WHAT MOTIVATES THIS TYPE OF KID?

All of us human beings have the need to be friends with our Creator. Some of us just deny it. Others accept it but don't make it a priority. The godly kid *does* make it a priority. Their motivation is "I want to get closer to God." They are like David, who wanted to dwell in God's house forever.

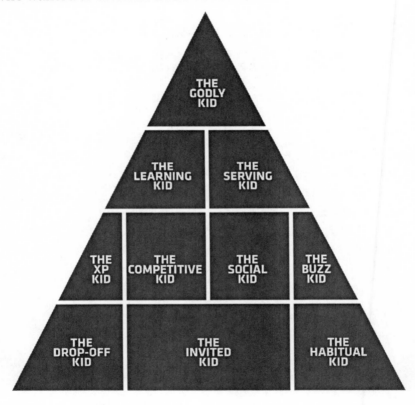

Note that this motivation can be temporary. Sometimes kids come to church tired or worried, and their desire to be close to God seems to have vanished. But they can be reminded of it easily, and will soften their hearts when God knocks. So don't be surprised when kids' motivations rise and drop from week to week. They're still kids, who can easily move with the waves of the wind. Look at the godly kid as a trend, not a weekly measurement.

In many cases, the godly kid is raised well and comes from a home where the parents place an emphasis on loving Christ. But this isn't always the case. Kids from any background can be a godly kid. Read Alvaro's amazing story.

CASE STUDY: ALVARO'S HUNGER FOR CHRIST

One time, my brother was at a Christian camp in Florida. The camp grounds were shared by a few churches. Sadly, my brother didn't find a lot of open hearts in his cabin group. But when he talked with kids from other cabins, he found a kid from Mexico, who wasn't raised a Christian at all. He was just sent over the border to attend a few camps and then to return to his family in Mexico.

The boy had a deep desire to learn about God—it was wild new stuff he was learning. He had a lifetime of learning to catch up on. So he didn't let my brother out of his sight and asked question after question. After days of this, the boy—named Alvaro—exclaimed that he wanted to be baptized. This was a challenge. The church my brother was with had a rule that kids could not be baptized unless their parents were present. Obviously, no parents are present at a camp, and the boy's parents were miles away. But my brother wasn't one to let ministry be stopped by restrictive policies that aren't in the Bible. He felt he had a Phillip-with-the-Ethiopian-official-moment, when the Ethiopian asked, "What's against it if I were baptized?" (Acts 8).

So he cooked up a plan for his young Mexican friend and talked with a youth pastor from another church at the camp. This pastor's church didn't have the ridiculous limitation, and he replied, "Well let's baptize him! I bet you if I asked my cabin, I'd have five boys who want to be baptized as well."

The pastor and my brother found the nearest water. It was a lake. Not far from there, kids were jumping off a blob and having all kinds of summer fun. The pastor's five boys got baptized right there, and so did Alvaro. He wanted his camp friends to be witnesses of this event, and the group was overjoyed. While they were baptizing, other kids saw what was happening and wanted to be baptized as well. A line began to form and joy began to spread. The pastor of my brother's church came upon the scene and blew a gasket. He shut it down immediately, and my brother was literally sat down to get a talking-to. It's funny how baptizing is controversial at a Christian camp. The pastor feared that parents would be livid because they weren't present at the baptism. Imagine that—the pastor was freaking out for the parents, even though no parent had freaked out just yet. Sadly this is the reality at many mega churches. At a large church, you'll always have an angry parent or two. And one angry parent can make the church set policies that will hinder future ministry.

To alleviate the situation, my brother said, "Why don't we call these kids' parents? If there's a problem, I'll be the first to apologize." The pastor didn't want my brother to call, so he called the parents of the kids himself. Each and every parent was overjoyed that their kid got baptized. One even said, "That's what I've been praying for." And as it so often goes, the angry pastor took the credit for what he'd been trying to stop all along. But that's fine. My brother never did it to get any credit. He did it for Alvaro. He did it for Jesus. Alvaro was a godly kid, and Efraim would not hinder his growth.

At the time of this writing, it's been seven years since this story. My brother is still in touch with Alvaro, and the angry youth pastor still serves at the mega church, which recently installed a new rule, "Kids may not accept Christ unless their parents are present."

It's been 2000 years since Jesus said, "Let the children come to me, do not hinder them," but these words still need to be said today.

NICK AND TANNER'S STORY

Yesterday I received a message from a teenager who wanted to talk face to face. I said that would be fine as long as he had his parents' permission, and told him I could Skype with him. He said that Skype is for old people and I should get this other app where you can talk with each other face to face, called HouseParty. I always listen to technology advice from kids, because it keeps me current. (Seven years ago some kid asked us to upload a YouTube video to teach them how to make videogames. Now we have over 60,000 followers. It's allowed us to talk about God to people from India to Pakistan to next door! Three years ago a kid at church installed the Instagram app for me, and it's been an incredible outreach tool. We now have over 6000 kids on there from around the world. One year ago a kid asked us to install...okay, you get the point. The moral of the story is that kids can be excellent technology advisors! Us church folks like to blame technology and block it out all too easily, burning the very bridges God puts at our disposal).

So I installed the app a while later, but the kid was not online. To my surprise the app had gone through all my contacts and added everyone who also had the app. Those kinds of things usually freak me out. If my phone breaks due to ministry, then it was a worthy sacrifice. To my second surprise all your "friends" in the app get to see you the moment you open it, and they get to talk to you without you having to accept a call from them.

So before I knew it, I was talking to a kid who had only been at our children's ministry two or three times and had now become a teenager. His name's Tanner. He told me to hold on, and a few seconds later, the screen split and one of his friends appeared on the face-call, surprising me a third time. Apparently friends of friends can join as well. Feeling that my privacy had shrunk to the size of a grain of sand, I composed myself and learnt that the new kid's name was Nick. After the introductions, Tanner said, "Ask him the questions, Nick. Ask him!"

It turned out that Nick was full of spiritual questions. Painfully so. There's no other way to say it than to say that he vomited questions. They almost came faster than I could answer them. And they weren't the easy ones either. "What's the difference between Catholics and "Christians?" (He didn't know the word Protestants.) "How do you get to heaven?" "Will I go to heaven?" "Do I really have to go to church?" We ended up talking for about an hour. The questions just kept coming. Toward the end, Nick said, "I just love this, I'm learning so much, all this knowledge is like, hitting my brain." Then the boys left and I nearly cried of joy.

Suddenly, out of nothing, an hour of deep ministry had happened. Needless to say, the godly kid (or the learning kid) was Nick, and kids like him can pop up at any time. All we have to do is allow God to interrupt us.

If you had seen Nick's face, you would've seen that the un-answered questions in his life were truly bothering him. Since you and I know the Bible so well, we are set free, and it's hard for us to imagine what it feels like when your heart is not free. And that doesn't just count for salvation. Any spiritual question can bug you and hold you prisoner until the day the question is answered. And that's what we get to do, you and I. This is what ministry is about!

WHEN THE QUESTIONS ERUPT AND TAKE OVER

Let me give you one last example showing how powerful it is when the learning kid and the godly kid enter your church and are given the freedom to ask questions.

You may remember me telling you about the "Life's Biggest Questions" series in chapter 9, in which we answer kids' hardest questions. Before we made that series, we were running some tests with lessons that would later turn into Life's Biggest Questions. During that user-test I made a little "mistake" on stage. I said, "Does anyone have any other questions?"

I just lit a fuse of a question-bomb, and it exploded in my face. And boy did the questions come! They weren't the questions where kids go, "Oh, sure, I'll ask something to make them happy." No, these were the, "I've always wanted to know this and my parents haven't been able to answer and it's been killing me inside," kind of questions.

I looked at the coordinator of the room. She was in charge. I knew what she was thinking, and she knew what I was thinking. She nodded, giving me permission to fully go off-script. I visibly dropped the paper, showing her I understood. For the next half-hour, all we did was answer questions. One after another. I would have broken down and cried like the leaders in the back, but God gave me enough adrenaline not to. After a while I allowed the kids to come closer to the stage and I sat down with them, answering one question after another. In this intimate setting, I could speak calmly and we all felt closer to our Maker.

While this was going on, the coordinator motioned to me. The parents had arrived. So I said to the kids, "I want to answer all of your questions, and I'll keep doing so until there are no more questions. While we do this, your parents will come in. If you want to go or have to go, you can. If you want to stay, you can stay."

The back doors were opened, and the parents walked in. Most of them were astonished and didn't want to break up what was going on. Some of them had their kids in hand, but stayed because they wanted to hear more answers for themselves and their kids as well. Some parents pushed their kids forward, whispering to them to ask certain questions. It took quite a while for the crowd to thin out, and some kids had to be dragged away by their parents, yelling, "Nooo, I have more questions!"

Once the room was empty, we evaluated and all said, "What just happened?" We were a Baptist church where everything is pretty much planned out. We joke that Baptists believe in the Holy Spirit, as long as he doesn't mess things up. Well, he sure did this time! In all honesty I did not believe that this could happen, but God clearly showed us what he was doing. And now that he had shown us, we could work with him and prepare for it.

In the following months we always had question times whenever we had time left. Sometimes kids would ask, "Is it time for questions yet?" The same phenomenon happened over and over again. Kids would already have their questions ready.

I'm telling you all this so that you too can plan for this to happen. I don't believe God only wants this to happen at one church. This is why it's important that we children's ministers share what God is doing, so that we can all be open for it.

So if the learning kids and the godly kids hijack your program, by all means, let them. In the gospels we see that half of Jesus' teachings were in response to what people were asking. So let them. And yes, it's nerve-wracking to have life's hardest questions thrown at you at lightning-speed. None of us think we have all the answers, and none of us do. But you can just answer with what you know, and find out what you don't know throughout the week. If God allows us, we'd love to write a book with all the questions kids ask and how we answer them. If you're interested in such a thing, drop us a line. For now, we have the "Life's Biggest Questions" series to help you answer the biggest ones.

PRO TIP: WHEN THE QUESTIONS STOP AS FAST AS THEY CAME

In order to be complete, I need to tell you of another interesting phenomenon. Sometimes when kids unleash a volley of questions, the questions suddenly stop. It's almost like someone flips an invisible switch and no more questions come. It's really funny to see and when it happened the first time, I asked

God what was going on, but he gave me peace about it. After training other leaders to answer questions, I told them about this and they noticed it as well.

The Bible describes the same phenomenon a couple times after people talk with Jesus. Luke 20 tells us, "And no one dared to ask him any more questions" (NIV, verse 40). Did they disagree? No, because it says, "Some of the scribes answered, 'Teacher, you have spoken well!'" So Jesus answers their questions well, they praise him for it, and they go quiet. The rich young man went away quietly as well (Luke 18:23, Mark 10:22, Matt. 19:22).

I'd love to hear your opinion, but here's what my leaders and I think is going on. The Holy Spirit, not us, draws people toward Christ. So when kids have questions, they're put in kids' hearts by the Holy Spirit. And when they're answered, kids begin to process them. This processing turns them quiet. I've seen it so many times now, it makes me happy. Some kids will burst out in praise, but many of them will go quiet. The answers are so deep and so clear—because God's Spirit speaks through you— that it turns their world upside down.

When I was a kid, we smuggled Bibles and tracts, and we once reached a village and gave the people a tract. The people began reading the tract while we were there. Usually there'd be many thank-you's and tears. This time was different. The people were so deeply into the tract, they forgot we were even there. When we drove off, we remarked that they didn't even see us leave. The messenger didn't matter—the message did. It had swooped into their world. The same goes for the kids who are absorbing the answers to the questions. It's more than kids thinking about a school assignment. Something deep and spiritual is going on in their hearts. They feel that light feeling of God pulling away the restrictions, flooding them with his insight. Could it be what Paul described when he said, "For the word of God is alive and active. Sharper than any double-edged sword, it penetrates even to dividing soul and spirit, joint and marrow" (Hebrew 4:12)?

In the USA we often want kids to be like cheerleaders. We want them to be wild and happy and ecstatic. But when God rocks a kid's world, allow him or her to be quiet. I call it the hourglass effect. You've just dumped all this new sand in the top, and they're slowly going to process it all. It takes mind, heart, and soul (Matthew 22:37). And once they've had time to process—without fail—kids will come back with more questions once the sand has gone through the middle. Almost every time I've seen kids leave in quiet processing-mode, I've seen them come back the next week with more questions. Because answered questions cause more questions. And that—as you already know—is just one sign of spiritual growth

AMPLIFYING THIS LEVEL OF MOTIVATION

How do you help the godly kids?

Well their motivation isn't something that you and I can cause to happen, obviously. It's the Holy Spirit within them. So the first thing to "help" this motivation is to pray. But you already knew that, so I didn't have to write it down. But I did, just so some wouldn't say, "You didn't mention prayer." So there. I mentioned prayer.

One other important thing to do is to affirm the godly kid's passion for Christ. Your connectors and roamers should already be doing that, but you can also do that from the stage. You've had the same experience as I have—that moment when you're teaching on stage and you're asking for an interaction or a response and there's this kid who responds with something so deep and profound it nearly knocks you off your feet.

You know that moment, right?

When that happens, first affirm that kid. Say whatever God has you say in that moment. I've said the craziest things:

- *"Becky, I want you to know how wise that answer was."* Boom. Maybe Becky isn't that good at school, but now she knows she's valued at church.

- *"Did you realize that you did not say that of yourself? God gave you this answer himself."* I've said this line many times. And yes, you can say that, because: "All wisdom comes from the Lord, and so do common sense and understanding" (Proverbs 2:6). So if a kid says something wise, it's from God. And Jesus said it to Peter as well, "Blessed are you, Simon son of Jonah! For this was not revealed to you by flesh and blood, but by My Father in heaven." I think I'm going to mention the kid's parent the next time as well, "Blessed are you, Rebecca, daughter of Lisa ..." or would I sound too much like Shakespeare? But all kidding aside, look at that compliment Jesus gives. That's absolutely amazing.

- *"Johnny, you are not far from the kingdom of God."* You can say this when kids almost get it and are really close. Jesus said it and he said we should be like him. So I say it when God has me say it.

- *"Wow, wow, wow. That was a deep insight. What is your name? John? Well I better remember that name because God might just use you for incredible things throughout your life. I believe that about you, John. Do you? Will you stay close to him for life? Okay."* When you say something like this, you're affirming them not just for now, but for their entire life. Notice the second half where you challenge them for a lifelong commitment. Here's how that usually plays out: during the compliment part you move closer to the kid. Then once you get to the commitment part, you point at the kid in order to put him in the spotlight and you physically start walking away. This way you make it feel like a "by the way." "By the way, will you follow God?" By walking away while asking something deep, you're showing everybody that this is just a normal thing to do and you can do so at any time. And the kid will never forget those few words you spoke.

Another version of a compliment is to give them a riddle or challenge. This is a fun method, picked up from the Master himself. (Yes, Jesus. Who else did you think I was referring to? Buddha?) After the rich young man answered Jesus wisely and correctly, Jesus gave the man a challenge by telling him to go and sell all he had. The same happened with Peter. Jesus once asked Peter three questions, and after each correctly-answered question, Jesus gave Peter a challenge in the form of a riddle: "Feed my lambs." "Take care of my sheep." "Feed my sheep" (John 21:15-19). What was Jesus' goal with these challenges? To give them a next step. To challenge them to grow further. In children's ministry we always give kids challenges. We tell them to learn a verse or to apply some scripture to their lives. But we rarely give a challenge just for one person. That's because it's not in the curriculum. But sometimes God may lead you to offer a challenge to a kid who is ready for a next step. Offer this challenge lovingly. In other trainings we talk about these challenges a bit more in-depth, but I wanted to mention it here so that you can experiment with it yourself. It's amazing.

Pray for the kid or for the subject he or she brought up. We were once playing a game with all the kids in the large room, and one kid yelled something to the extent of "This is SO much fun!" In that moment I felt really grateful for God to give us this much fun so I said, "Everybody freeze! While you're frozen, we should realize that she was right. This is tons of fun. Do you guys agree?" Kids agreed through their "frozen" mouths, and I continued, "And God has given us this fun and he loves it when we thank him for it. So let's thank him real quick." The prayer was a short three-sentence praise to God, and then we continued. This teaches kids that whatever they say can influence the program. It teaches them that God speaks through them as well. It also teaches them that you can pray to God at any time, not just at planned moments (the beginning and end of a service, bedtime, and dinner, for example).

Once, after I'd given a deep question to the crowd, a girl gave an incredibly wise answer, and I just felt the Holy Spirit tell me to affirm her, so I said, "Hey, guys, I want everybody to know what's happening right now because this is amazing." I told her that I felt God had a big plan for her life, that I felt the same for all of the kids present, but in that moment I wanted her to know that she wasn't far from the kingdom of God, which Jesus tells us about. I asked her if she wanted to end our time with a prayer, since it was close to the end of the service. She prayed an amazing prayer. After the prayer, it was hard for me not to cry because it was so magnetic; after the service, I just kept talking with her and affirmed her. Years later, she felt called to be a ministry leader. She was a godly kid for sure.

We amplify the godly kids by praying for God to stir in the hearts of our kids, by affirming them deeply, by giving them challenges and riddles that help them grow further, and by praying spontaneously as a response to what kids do and say. The last method is to make the godly kids the heroes in the room.

Whenever kids are hungry for God's word and whenever you see that hunger at any time or in any setting, affirm them immediately and as publicly as possible, and by doing so you make those kids the heroes, and then the whole group of kids will want to be like them. Then you've truly begun to reach your goal—you're highlighting the top of the pyramid, the highest level of commitment. You're highlighting the kids in your ministry who want to become like Jesus.

One word of caution here: When you turn these kids into an example, don't do it in such a way that you make them exceptional, because if you say, "In ten years of children's ministry, I've never seen this," then you are basically telling all of the other kids that they cannot reach this same level. What you want to do is make them the hero in such a way that *everyone* can be a hero just like them.

Make them the example to be like, not the exception to be in awe of.

NOTES

How this works: Once you find the answers in the chapter, you can note them here for future reference. Also capture your own ideas. You'll often get ideas while reading, which you'll never think of again. So capture them now and implement them over time!

1. Motivation 10 = the g_____ kid
2. Their motivation is: "I want _____
   _____"
3. Ways to amplify this motivation:

4. Your own ideas to amplify this motivation:

TAKING THINGS FURTHER

TEAM QUESTIONS

Note: The team questions do more than revisit what's taught in the chapter. They help you to take things further than the chapter did. Some things are better discovered by yourself, and as a team. Wouldn't you agree?

1. At 12-years-old, Jesus said, "Didn't you know I had to be in my Father's house?" That's about the only message we hear from Jesus at 12. Could that mean that this is the most important message for teenagers?

2. Which kids in your ministry are the godly kids? Which of them truly want to be close to God? (Remember, there can be wiggle room in this motivation from week to week. Some weeks they're less motivated than others, but look at the overall trend—the average—per kid.)

3. Alvaro's story showed us how church policies can be an obstacle for the godly kid. Which rules has your ministry set that could stop spontaneous ministry from happening? Many policies are made due to one or two exceptional cases, but the policy then squashes ministry going forward. What policies could you loosen?

4. Nick and Tanner's story is a prime example of a kid whose questions come up at a random time. How can you be available to kids and families when their questions come up? These questions will come up. Do you want it to be you who is there to field those questions, or someone who will give secular answers?

5. Have you ever allowed the Holy Spirit to take over the program and do something you didn't expect? Is it scary to step onto the unscripted path and veer away from the

curriculum? Would you like more divine interruptions? (Remember: you can always connect back to the curriculum at any point after the interruption!)

6. Have you seen kids fall quiet after asking questions? Did you spot them reaching a temporary point of saturation? (Note: this rarely happens during regular programming. It does happen when they are free to ask whatever question they want).

7. Have you seen kids who got questions answered and asked more questions as a result of answered questions? How could you have this happen more? One way I do it is by answering questions in such a way that a new door opens. So each response answers the asked question, but also introduces a new mystery (Colossians 1:27).

8. Pray for a groundswell of love for Christ among kids in your ministry and outside in your region. Pray for the news to spread through the region like in the gospels. Ask that God will surpass your team's highest goals. "I am doing something in your days—you would not believe if you were told" (Hab. 1:5 NASB).

Chapter 12
ALL MOTIVATIONS MATTER

IF YOU LOOK AT THE BOTTOM LAYER of the triangle, it's all external motivation: the drop-off kid, the invited kid, the habitual kid—these kids are all being motivated by someone else, who brought them there. And that's fine for now.

The level above that is all internal motivation. Kids are motivated on their own. The experience kid, the competitive kid, the social kid, and the buzz kid—they all come because of their own motivation. But it's still not a spiritual motivation. Not yet.

And then, on the top level, we have our spiritual motivation. The learning kid, the serving kid, and the godly kid—they all want to get closer to Christ.

We obviously want all kids to have the highest level of motivation, to be the godly kids. And when we look at a lower level of motivation, such as the buzz kid, we feel that their motivation isn't worth that much. After all, that one isn't a spiritual motivation. It's just a kid who goes for whatever is cool at the moment. What good does that do?

But it really doesn't matter what motive kids have to come to church. When Jesus walked on earth, many came to him just to see him do some miracles. They came for "magic tricks" not for the message. But how many of those who came for the hype were eventually captured by the life-changing message?

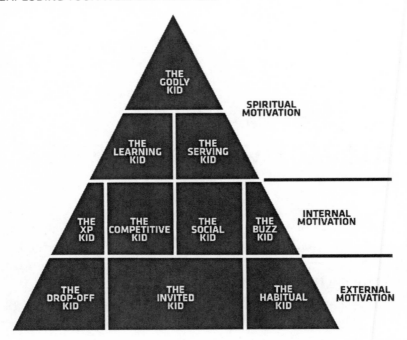

In youth ministry, I've often connected with new boys who came in, and I knew exactly what they came for. My conversation with them would go like this:

"Hey, what's up? Welcome! I'm Ruben."

"Hi, I'm John."

"Hi, John, nice to meet you. Is this your first time here?"

"Yeah."

"Bro, you're gonna have so much fun. I don't wanna exaggerate, but it's gonna be the best day of your life, I betcha. It's gonna be better than the day you were born. It's that epic here."

(laughs) "Sure."

"So what made you wanna come today?"

"I dunno."

"What's her name?"

(laughs shyly) "Uh, I dunno."

"Don't worry, I won't tell."

(laughs) "Abby."

"I love your honesty."

(laughs again) "Thanks."

"Well, I wish you the best of luck. Oh by the way, at your age these relationships last three weeks at most, don't they?"

(laughs again) "That's so true."

"In case yours does, we'll be here for you once your heart is all broken and stuff, hmkay?"

"Haha, okay."

"And while you're here, you might just find something you weren't looking for. Something that lasts your entire life."

"I guess."

"Well I better get lost, 'cause you're a man on a mission. I'll catch up with you later, hmkay?"

"Okay, cool."

Now, this is obviously a youth ministry conversation and not a children's ministry conversation, but it illustrates a couple good points. First of all, I didn't blame the new kid for why he came to church. To me, there's plenty wrong with his motivation. I'm not a big proponent of girlfriend/boyfriend behavior at a young age, let alone between Christians and non-Christians. But John came to church. He had decided that his passion for a girl was strong enough that he would get over his fear of whatever this church is, and he'd come in so he could see her. And maybe part of him was curious about church as well—how would I know? Who am I to judge? In my little conversation with him, I was able to establish some deep trust in seconds, and I was able to invite him to explore what church has to offer. In an indirect way, I was able to tell him, "I accept you, and there's more for you here once you feel free to look further than you are looking now."

I can't tell you how often I've had this type of conversation in youth ministry and it's a great bridge to more meaningful conversations later. In fact, last weekend I had this conversation with a student called Aeden. The girl he liked did not show up at church and he felt lost. So I hung out with him throughout the service and the two of us had a great and long conversation. (For the record, yes, we talk during the service! Give your roamers and connectors the authority to talk during the service!) I started off teaching him how to treat girls with respect, because that's what interested him. You always start where they are. He absolutely loved to learn how to be a gentleman and from his responses, it was clear that his parents never taught him about that. This conversation gained his trust at a rapid pace and before I knew it, he was asking advice on many life situations that plagued him, told me how he's scared of his father from time to time, how his relationship with his mother was rocky, and even confessed that he was a bad brother to his siblings. In 30 minutes there was more honesty spilling out of Aedan than I've seen spill out of many lifelong Christian kids. His motivation to be at church had changed in less than a minute, and he's coming again next week.

The moral of the story is that it's not up to us to judge people's motivations. That's not our job. Our job is to start where kids are, and entice them to take a good look at what Christ has to offer. It's our privilege to become their friends, and introduce them to our best friend, whom they cannot yet see.

If you think about it, did you first come to Christ with purely selfless motivations? Not even close. In fact, without God's Spirit within you, you were not even capable of being 100 percent selfless. So if kids come for the buzz, it's great. If kids come because they want to win a prize, that's an okay start. It's up to your connectors and roamers to foster friendships that stand out in their lives. Friendships that lead them by hand, toward the throne of their Maker.

HOW TO IMPLEMENT ALL THESE CHANGES WITH-OUT BURNING OUT

Okay, great—so all motivations matter. But there are 10 of the and each has many creative ways to implement them. And I bet you and your team have come up with even more ideas on how to implement them. So if you look at all of those new ideas, it might just be a little overwhelming to do them all.

I would advise you not to implement them all at once. It will cause a storm of new activity that may not be sustainable. They key is to implement more and more over time, without losing sight of it, and adding these ideas to your ongoing "system."

Here some tips on how to do that:

1. First, read this book with your team, if you haven't yet. It's important to begin by thinking along the same lines. Just like a piece of metal can become a magnet when the individual magnetic moments of the atoms are aligned, your team will become a powerful force when your thinking aligns. To help you with that, use the group questions at the end of each chapter. You can discuss those together. They don't only reiterate what's in a chapter; they also help you think further than what the chapter discussed.

2. By going over the questions together, you'll already be implementing many of the items together. You'll also get to discover who is passionate about which motivation.

3. After each chapter, you saw two squares in the notes section. In one square, note what the chapter said you could implement; in the other square, note the ideas you and your team come up with. Then afterwards, tally up all the ideas from all the chapters and make a giant map.

4. Now look at that map and prioritize which ideas you'll implement first, and which you'll implement later. You can make a schedule, implementing a few each month, or you could designate "champions," individuals who will oversee the implementation of specific ideas. If your team doesn't have enough champions yet, some tasks can wait until you do.

A MINISTRY THAT SERVES YOUR MINISTRY

Your church is full of talented people, and some are just naturally great at spreading ideas and promoting things. Creative communication is a gift, and those who have it are rarely called upon by the church. But your children's ministry can do just that!

Maybe you'll want to take the ideas from this book and have a small team (or even just one person, for starters) run with it. Their sole purpose is to help get the word out about your children's ministry and to help you make your ministry accessible. You could call them the promotion team or the hospitality team. Give them the authority to be anywhere at your children's ministry to evaluate how things are going. Because hospitality and promotion are so much more than putting up a few posters; they help you turn the ministry into something worth talking about.

As you have seen in this book, some of the ideas are promotion-related (such as giving out spreadables), and some ideas are directly related to how you do ministry. For instance, if you have roamers who build deep friendships with the kids, then you haven't done any promotion, but you certainly made kids more likely to attend. Your promotional team could serve the children's ministry team and hold you accountable to have you become the most accessible children's ministry you can be.

When it comes to the promotional side of things, your hospitality team could take care of trailers, after-service activities, T-shirts, armbands, or challenges. They'll work closely with you because it directly affects your team. If you can assemble a good team to tackle these kinds of things, it could really help your ministry. Stuff like this may not be your gifting, but it may be theirs.

It's important to recognize that some people have a gift of very creative communication, and if you can have these people on your side, do it—because these are also gifts that God gives us that are not often used at the church. Sometimes these people may feel their gifts can't be used for God just because the church isn't tapping into it—but you can. If change can happen anywhere in the church, it's in children's and youth ministry. Kids don't complain about change the way adults do. In fact, they welcome it.

My father was a pastor for 32 years, and whenever he wanted to make a change, he started in his children's and youth ministry and then bumped it up to the adults later, rather than the other way around. He would say, "Your kids are already doing this," and then the adults would do it too.

Your ministry could easily become the leading edge in innovation for your church.

WORKS IN PROGRESS

Before I finish, I want to let you know about some more resources we're compiling to help you improve your children's and youth ministries. This book is more about what makes kids come to church. The next one we're working on discusses what keeps them at church, and that delves into those relationships we were talking about earlier, working with connectors and roamers and so forth. We'll show you how to foster these relationships in your ministry and what goals to give your volunteers as well as talk a little more about ways you can get them from standing in the back to really engaging with the kids. That will be coming soon. If you'd like, you can go to KidsWantAnswers.com and drop us your email so we can keep you up to date on all of the things we do, from video trainings to informational books, story series, or curriculums like the ones we discussed earlier.

I hope you found this little book useful. I've really enjoyed giving all of this, which God gave us, back to the body of Christ. I love you guys dearly, even if I don't know you, and I pray for all the ministries out there because we are really at a tipping point in children's and youth ministry.

We're either going after our culture as we go after Christ, or we're not.

CAN I PRAY FOR YOU?

God, thank you so much for these men and women who put their lives in your hands to reach the youngest generation. Lord, I pray you make us become like kids, just as you said that we should, so that we can reach them and also learn from them because they're the body of Christ as well. Thank you so much for this deeply privileged work that you give us to do every day. It's so meaningful and so valuable. Lord, turn all these kids into learning kids, serving kids, and godly kids because we want to see them lifting up your name and serving in your kingdom. Amen.

God bless you guys, and have a great time putting some of these ideas into practice. Contact me anytime to let me know how things are going: info@kidsWantAnswers.com. We're in this together.

NOTES

Best Friends For Life
How to live the most meaningful life together

This series is specifically designed for *the serving kid, the learning kid, the Godly kid and the invited kid.*

These seven jam-packed curriculum lessons for ages 6-12, teach kids how to transform their existing groups of friends into change-makers!

Challenge your kids to go out and transform their community for Christ, just like in the book of Acts!

Life's Biggest Questions
...about God

Series of (5) Children's Programs | Ages 6-12

LIFE'S BIGGEST
QUESTIONS

...nswers.com

KIDSWANTANSWERS.COM/LBQ

This series is specifically designed for the
learning kid, and answers kids' most-asked questions about God.
These questions are rarely ever answered in Children's ministry, so get ready for a
jolt of enthusiasm from the kids.
With a unique "leave-them-guessing-for-a-while" type program flow, kids learn
how to know that God exists, why God is invisible, how it could be that bad
things happen even if God loves them, and more.

David 1 & 2
How to be a leader

Both of these 5-week series help kids to become
deeply immersed in the life of David.
With cutting edge full-feature animations, you will take kids through the book of
1st Samuel; from when we first hear of David to when he's crowned king over
Judah. They'll learn what made David such a great leader that God called him "a
man after God's own heart."
**Kids can even unlock a videogame of David's life and give their feedback to
the twins, who are developing the game of David!**
These series have been a vision for over 10 years, and the twins are incredibly

Future Spies

Our most ambitious series yet! "Future spies" is a curriculum series that contains a weekly story, jam-packed with comedy, nail-biting tension, amazing characters and mind-blowing plot twists. Your kids will follow four kid-spies. While they carry out their secret missions, they come upon a conspiracy bigger than themselves, and are forced to work together, all they while discovering what it really means to live a "life of service".

Life's Biggest Questions 2

The next "Life's Biggest Questions" series dives into kids' biggest questions about Jesus. Was he just a man? How do we know that he was who we think he is? What was his big message? Who did Jesus himself think that he was? Kids will discover the most engaging story of our savior, and they'll go way beyond merely understanding sin and salvation. They'll learn the entire narrative of the Bible and how Jesus plays the central role inside of it.

Choices

Kids are always told to make the right choices. But how exactly do you do that? This series gives kids 7 steps to make even the hardest choices together with God. From simple things like, "What should I do today?" to hard ones like, "What school should I choose?" and "Which parent should I live with?". Kids will learn a Biblical guide to involve God in their decision-making... for life!

For more TornadoTwins curriculum,
videogames, books and movies, visit:

KIDSWANTANSWERS.COM